SESAME STREET DAD

Evolution of an Actor

A MEMOIR

by

ROSCOE ORMAN

PORTLAND • OREGON

Copyright © 2006 by Roscoe Orman

Cover and interior design by Masha Shubin
Cover photo © Roscoe Orman
Back portrait © Richard Termine

Sesame Street and associated characters, trademarks and design elements are owned and licensed by Sesame Workshop. © 2006 Sesame Workshop. All rights reserved.

All rights reserved. No part of this book may be reproduced or transmitted in any form or by any means whatsoever, including photocopying, recording or by any information storage and retrieval system, without written permission from the publisher. Contact Inkwater Press at 6750 SW Franklin Street, Suite A, Portland, OR 97223-2542.

www.inkwaterpress.com

Paperback
ISBN-10 1-59299-210-2
ISBN-13 978-1-59299-210-2

Hardback
ISBN-10 1-59299-213-7
ISBN-13 978-1-59299-213-3

Publisher: Inkwater Press

Printed in the U.S.A.

MEMOIR

The pores of life's vast membrane
Overflow with a rapid fluid mix
Of memory
And fill the page, retained
Recalled, forgotten, and stirred
Remixed, discarded, and recovered
All there but in a new light
Imbued with the shadow play
Of time's wise vision
And age's urgent prodding
Reviewed and refined for consumption
By the curious and concerned
Deposited in archival sanctity,
Posthumously revived,
Revisited again and again
To be reborn in the hearts
Of future ages.

9/30/03

To Hunter, Nanny, and Mom

Acknowledgments

THE UNDERTAKING AND COMPLETION of the task of writing this book would not have been realized without the help and support of various friends, family members, and colleagues whose input to this work is immeasurable. There are many whose contributions will go unmentioned, but suffice it to say that most of the people whose names appear within these pages have had, even if unknowingly, some impact upon their content. There are some, however, whose direct assistance to me in this project cannot go unrecognized. To my dear friend and editor Karen Allen Baxter, words are insufficient to express my gratitude to you for three decades of friendship and support and for helping to make this book more than just a collection of facts and dates. Likewise, to literary agent Marie Brown. Your extraordinary expertise and patience have been invaluable in propelling this project beyond what I had originally thought possible. To editors Khadijah Caturani and William Lee, your insights and your generosity have added significantly to the quality of this work. To Bill and Melvina Lathan, St. Clair Bourne, Gary James, Tommy Hicks, Count and Amianna Stovall, Erik Lewis, John O'Neal, Ademola Olugebefola, Gary Bolling, and Michael White, your comments and/or suggestions, not to mention your fellowship, have been, as always, deeply appreciated. To all my friends at Inkwater Press, especially Virginia Martin, Jeremy Solomon, Masha Shubin, and Linda Weinerman, thank you so much for believing in my work and for helping me turn this long-held dream into beautiful reality. To my mom, Viola Bernice Queeley, thanks for the great family photos and also for giving me life *and* the ability to enjoy it. To my children Rasheda, Solana, Miles, and Cheyenne and grandchildren Darryl, Nautica, Richmond, Jaden, and Nyla, thanks for being my pride and joy as well as my primary inspiration for telling this story. And to my wife, Sharon Joiner Orman, thanks for providing this story and my life with true meaning.

R.O.

Table of Contents

Acknowledgments • vii
Introduction • xi

CHAPTER ONE
First Steps • 1

CHAPTER TWO
Southern Journey • 25

CHAPTER THREE
The Prodigal Son Returns • 45

CHAPTER FOUR
Moving On • 71

CHAPTER FIVE
Sowing (Sesame) Seeds • 81

CHAPTER SIX
Reaping the Harvest • 89

CHAPTER SEVEN
Mastery • 97

CHAPTER EIGHT
Maturation • 115

CHAPTER NINE
Sesame Kaleidoscope • 123

CHAPTER TEN
Middle Passage • 139

CHAPTER ELEVEN
New Vistas • 147

CHAPTER TWELVE
Toward the Light • 161

CHAPTER THIRTEEN
Regeneration • 183

Index List • 196
Index of Photographs • 208

Introduction

THERE ARE SEVERAL COMPELLING reasons why I wrote this book. First and foremost, I wanted to pass along to my children and their fellow "hip-hop-generation-Xers" information which might serve as a series of historical reference points to help illuminate the paths that their own lives may follow. Given a cultural heritage defined by a lack of knowledge about its own antiquity, I also know relatively little about the lives of my own immediate forebears, not to mention those who preceded them. Realizing, however, the valuable lessons that can be learned from each of our journeys by those who come after us, I am compelled to help close the information gap between my generation and my children's. Although still vigorously engaged in what has been a lifelong quest for self-discovery and artistic growth, I am inspired by the hope that my own personal path up to this point, my explorations, struggles, and accomplishments might be interesting, informative, and useful to an emerging generation in the process of defining the world on its own terms. Given that each new age must follow a course suited to its own current demands, I offer my story in a spirit of generosity, joy, hope, and compassion as a voice from the recent past and present to the open ears of the future.

The disparate paths that we each take, although connected by universal themes and common experiences, are so uniquely individualized that unless we assume the task of telling our own stories in our own words they can be easily misinterpreted by others. This book, which hopefully includes the spiritual tenor of my times as well as the philosophical and educational enrichment I have received within them, is a distinctly personal account and interpretation of my life experiences that may also serve as a lasting record of the events described, many of which have historical significance beyond my own personal story.

The four decades which my career has thus far spanned encompass a period of change that is unprecedented in the history of American society, particularly in regards to race relations and the impact of African-American culture on popular culture. The seeds of this revolution, sown by the horrifying Middle Passage and by more than four centuries of barbarous slavery and oppression and cultivated by twentieth century developments such as the Great Northern Migration, the Niagara Movement, the Harlem Renaissance, the various ages of Jazz, the Blues, the WPA Projects, the seminal works of Dr. W.E.B. DuBois, the moral and intellectual courage of Paul Robeson, the mythic feats of Jack Johnson, Joe Louis, Jesse Owens, and Jackie Robinson in sports, and the triumph of Brown v. the Board of Education; these and other examples of socio-cultural progress inspired the generations of intellectuals, artists, athletes, social activists, and others who have worked toward the pursuit of human advancement and equality. It was this legacy which I and my contemporaries fell heir to at the dawn of the 1960s and which has, subsequently, informed much of the quality and content of my life as actor, father, husband, teacher, and writer.

It is also my intention to further illuminate and validate for the reader a career defined in large part by its association with *Sesame Street,* a television program whose enormous reputation and impact have sometimes overshadowed the individual contributions of many connected with the show over a long period of time, as well as our careers outside and beyond the show. Certainly, my three decades as Gordon on *Sesame Street* have provided one of the most enriching and edifying stories of my life. If I could boast of no other major career accomplishment, having played a central role as I have in the development and continuation of this landmark series would alone have made my life sufficiently meaningful. The historical significance of *Sesame Street* and its surprising longevity have made my association with the show, in many regards, my life's crowning achievement. Reviewing the entirety of my career, however, has given me an opportunity to examine the political, moral, social, cultural, and artistic connections and influences that have defined *all* its aspects. Within the realm of theater, for instance, it is clear that my early affiliations with The Free Southern Theater of New Orleans and The New Lafayette Theatre of Harlem between the mid-1960s and the early 1970s have been, arguably, even more influential in defining the content of my personal character *and* my life's work than have my many years as Gordon. This is not to mention my first twenty years of life, the richly mentored, Bronx-bred childhood and adolescence which laid the entire foundation for all that was to follow.

From the very onset of a well-seasoned journey through the worlds of theater, television, and film, it has always been the inherent value within the material I have chosen to perform, the institutions to which I have become attached, and the individuals with whom I have been associated which have invariably dictated those choices, underwritten the overall effectiveness of my forty years of professional work, and given me a sense of fulfillment. It is the *entirety* of that story and its cumulative influence upon me that I wish to share with the reader.

...and film, it...
...been the inherent value...
...erial I have chosen to perform, the...
...which I have become attached, and the individu...
...whom I have been associated which have inva...
...dictated those choices, underwritten the ov...
effectiveness of my forty years of professio...
...and given me a sense of fulfillment. It is...
...irety of that story and its cumulative influe...
...me that I wish to share with the reader.

Chapter One
First Steps

"Grandpa Superman, Grandpa Superman!" The wor...
...at me with such unbridled enthusiasm that...
...n't quite know how to respond. With a look...
...eful recognition, they had come out of the mo...
...my four year-old grandson Richmond as he and...
...ther Jaden, a year and a half younger, sat in...
...r seat of my car. I hadn't seen them since Ja...
...beginning to walk just over a year ago and...
...looking forward to having them stay with th...
...ndma Sharon, their Aunt Cheyenne, and me for a...
...ks. Although I hadn't seen them, they had watc...
(even though they lived hundreds of miles away...
...anta, Georgia) on their TV as Gordon of Ses...
...eet for as long as they could remember. And wi...
...the past two years Gordon had taken on a brand...
...sona as "Trash" Gordon, the favorite superhero...
...ar the Grouch and his pet worm Slimy. Most e...
...es of the show now ended with Oscar reading Sl...
...chapter from the adventures of the interg...
...rior who fights against the ev...
...ch-infested univer...

BIRTH

It aint simple
what you feel
or how well you do it
to be for real / is you
so deep a meal
for me / it's true
& everything I've seen
is in this moment
(catch y'r breath)
the sun is in y'r eyes
explodin' in you &
the babyman is comin'
outside-inside-out
hold on &
jes' push love
of loves
then lay.

11/27/74

"Grandpa Superman, Grandpa Superman!" The words came at me with such unbridled enthusiasm that I didn't quite know how to respond. With a look of gleeful recognition, they had come out of the mouth of my four-year-old grandson Richmond as he and his brother Jaden, a year and a half younger, sat in the back seat of my car. I hadn't seen them since Jaden was beginning to walk just over a year ago and I was looking forward to having them stay with their Grandma Sharon, their Aunt Cheyenne, and me for a few weeks. Although *I* hadn't seen *them*, *they* had watched *me* (even though they lived hundreds of miles away in Atlanta, Georgia) on their TV as Gordon of *Sesame Street* for as long as they could remember. And within the past two years Gordon had taken on a brand new persona as "Trash" Gordon, the favorite superhero of Oscar the Grouch and his pet worm Slimy. Most episodes of the show now ended with Oscar reading Slimy another chapter from the adventures of the intergalactic warrior who fights against the evils of a grouch-infested universe. Hence, Richmond's reaction upon seeing me for the first time in a year was one of utter amazement, awe, and near worship. Not only was I Grandpa but Superman as well, as proven by his repeated sightings of me wearing my superhero suit, cape and all, slaying villains in faraway galaxies. In my own heart and mind, however, his response signaled a new and deeper level of success in my life, in that I would now and forever be remembered by him and his brother as truly "super," making them, as my grandsons, equally "super." "Yes," I thought (only half jokingly), "my legacy is now complete."

People often ask me what I am most proud of about my association with *Sesame Street*. In this, my thirty-second anniversary year of playing Gordon Robinson, it strikes me that what the character most significantly symbolizes, his most distinguishing and praiseworthy attribute, may lie in the simple fact that he is a man of African descent who for over three decades has been a respected and beloved father figure to young people of all races and all social classes all across America and beyond. Although born in a country that was founded and has continued to thrive upon the subjugation of his ancestors, he harbors no hatred or thirst for revenge but, on the contrary, is a model of patience, understanding, and civic responsibility who embraces all of humankind. He has, in fact, gained audiences' affections not for being the wealthiest, most famous, the most athletically endowed or powerful black man in America (despite "Trash" and the occasional delusion on my part of being such) but, instead, for his sensitivity, intelligence, lack of guile, and his enduring ability to be everyone's friend (even Oscar the Grouch). All of these virtues, especially in marital partnership with Susan, Loretta Long's exemplary model of African-American womanhood, stand in sharp contrast to the prevailing images of black men that have been projected within mainstream American culture since and especially prior to *Sesame Street*'s premiere and certainly during the formative years of my own generation. Although I can claim only a small portion of the credit for what the character of Gordon represents (he was, after all, conceived by the program's founders Joan Ganz Cooney and Jon Stone and played by two other actors before me, most notably Matt Robinson, one of the show's early writer-producers), it is nonetheless, a character who has had an immeasurable impact on the lives of millions of people under the age of forty and one which, amid a multitude of other roles in my career, I've come to feel that I was probably born to play.

That birth, of Roscoe Hunter Orman, occurred on the 11th day of June in 1944 at Columbia Presbyterian Hospital in the Washington Heights neighborhood of New York City, five days after D-Day when the Allied forces invaded Normandy, thus beginning the liberation of Europe and foretelling the end of World War II. My father, Roscoe Irving Orman, was a transplanted native of Tampa, Florida, who, with no training or professional experience, was considered by many among family, friends, and acquaintances as a naturally gifted athlete, singer, dancer, and all-around entertainer. As a young husband and father he

My maternal grandparents, Hunter and Nanny Wells, 1956.

My father, Roscoe Irving Orman in uniform, 1945.

Stepfather Eddie Queeley and Mom, 1960.

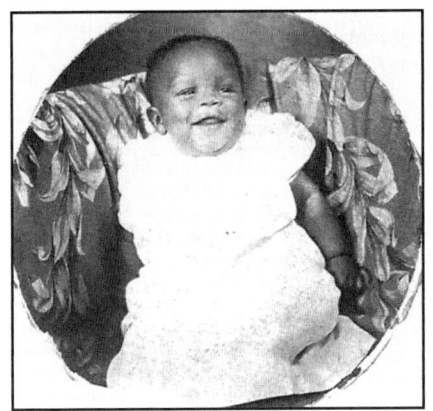

Me in my Christmas gown at 5 months, 1944.

Mom with me at age two, 1946.

Me and Cookie in my godmother Connie Mitchell's wedding, 1947.

Me and Mobo, 1951.

went off to serve in that "good war" and, like so many soldiers throughout history, never fully recovered from the emotional and psychological trauma of the experience. Along with countless other black American servicemen who had fought against the forces of fascism abroad, he returned home to a country which denied him anything even resembling sufficient recognition for the sacrifices he had made on its behalf. To make matters worse, while serving he was introduced to morphine, leading to what would eventually become a life-long struggle with drug addiction. By the time I was three, he and my mother, Viola Bernice, had divorced, leaving her and her parents to care for my younger sister Rochelle and me.

That same year the family moved out of the house on Tinton Avenue near 163rd Street, just a stone's throw away from Yankee Stadium, where I had spent my first three years of life. We relocated a few miles north to an apartment house in the bustling, multi-ethnic (predominately Jewish), post-war Bronx neighborhood on Stebbins Avenue near Boston Road and within two blocks of beautiful Crotona Park. I have only a few vague memories of life on Tinton Avenue with both of my parents, mostly revolving around their full and active social life with friends, food, and the sounds of mid-1940s be-bop music around the house. On the other hand, my next eight years of life at 1415 Stebbins Avenue contained many memorable moments of great friendships, a vibrant community life, and close family ties. They were the years of summer street games like stickball, skelly, ring-o-leevio, and kick the can; of Cub Scout meetings, Sunday school, play streets and block parties; of homemade scooters and of penny candies and egg creams at the corner store.

Naturally, the absence of my father had a profound effect upon my early childhood years. Extremely shy, I was slow learning how to speak and developed a severe stutter which, with the help of special remedial classes, greatly improved during my first few years of grade school. In all likelihood, the attention to diction and elocution during these sessions both boosted my self-confidence in speaking and also provided me with some basic skills that would come into play later as I tried my hand at acting. I've been told, in fact, that Rochelle, fourteen months my junior, was responsible for much of my early language development. Rochelle, known as Cookie (I was Ricky) has always been and remains the superior talker.

Given my father's absence, I was extremely fortunate to have had a male role model in my maternal grandfather Hunter Edmund Wells, a master chef, chauffeur, and professional handyman, whom we all called Hunter. Born in Powhattan, Virginia, a small farming community outside of Richmond in 1905, Hunter spent much of his childhood being shuttled back and forth between the family farm in Virginia and Harlem, New York, where his parents had migrated in search of a better life. In spite of his receiving only a third-grade education, he would acquire, through the school of "hard knocks" and his innate intelligence and creativity, a multitude of skills which would serve him well during his lifetime. An avid outdoorsman who loved to hunt and fish, Hunter was both a "man's man" and a dashingly handsome gentleman who could charm any lady in sight.

In Viola Moore, Hunter had met his match. A second-generation New Yorker born in 1906, Nanny belonged to a family whose descendants had migrated from England with solid beliefs in education and social self-improvement. She and Hunter had grown up in the same Harlem neighborhood where she decided at the age of thirteen that they were destined for one another. They were, indeed, the "perfect" pair. Together they became members of Harlem's Les Modernes Bridge Club as well as champion ballroom dancing partners, with Nanny's prim and proper ways a well-fitting complement to Hunter's relaxed and jovial gregariousness.

Mom, or "Baby" as she was and still is affectionately called by all but her children, was the younger of the two Wells daughters. Her older sister Margaret had, by the age of twenty-two, become entrapped within what would become a long, unhappy marriage with seven children. Contrastingly, when Baby's comparatively short marriage to Roscoe ended, she stayed close to her "empty nested" parents who were still relatively young and willing to help her raise their two small grandchildren. Having Nanny available as a stay-at-home childcare provider enabled Mom to secure a variety of jobs during her child-rearing years, including dry cleaning press operator, laminator of city records, proof machine operator for Federal Reserve Bank, and head receptionist at the Bronx's Jacobi Hospital's Psychiatric Division. These work experiences coupled with her youthfulness (she was seventeen when I was born), her inbred common sense, and the cheerful nature which she inherited from Hunter all helped form Mom's approach to parenthood. Far from the strict disciplinarian that Nanny had been with her and Margaret (and to some extent with Cookie and me), Mom was able to convey to her children the deeper meanings of morality and reason without the use of the antiquated dictums which had been a part of her own childhood ("Children should be seen and not heard, etc."). Without the benefit of having read Dr. Spock, Mom was way ahead of her time in her understanding and use of child psychology. A typical response to one of my acts of boyhood mischief (such as the time that best friend Larry Satchell and I wandered off from Stebbins Avenue on our roller skates to explore a strange new neighborhood, not returning until after dark) would be first an expression of anger or frustration over what I had done in order to get my attention (only rarely accompanied by a spanking), immediately followed by a calm and sensible explanation of why she had become upset. These brief emotional outbursts on Mom's part would seemingly take more of a toll on her than on me and, coupled with her reasoned approach afterward, would tell me both that she cared deeply about my conduct *and* that she respected my ability to think and learn how to monitor my own behavior. Such intrinsic lessons throughout my childhood became the foundation of my own approach to parenting and to life in general.

Whatever talents I have as a performer were inherited, like my first and middle names, from men on both sides of the family. Family members loved telling me about Roscoe's legendary exploits as a dancer, performer, and perpetual "life of the party." In addition, Hunter, who sang with a sweetly melodic high-tenor voice and was the best tune whistler I've ever heard, often shared anecdotes and reenactments with me of his experiences as a vaudeville song-and-dance man in 1920s Harlem. He was especially proud of having performed at the famed Lafayette Theatre with the highly regarded actress Abby Mitchell. Hunter took great delight in describing an episode backstage in which the resourceful Miss Mitchell came to his rescue during a severe case of laryngitis by finger forcing a wad of Vaseline down his constricted throat.

My first recollection of performing before an audience (other than my family) occurred within the first few weeks of attending kindergarten at Public School 54. For reasons which I can't recall, I somehow found myself in front of Mrs. Frederick's entire class singing a heartfelt rendition of "That Lucky Ole Sun," a song made famous in the late 1940s by popular balladeer Frankie Laine which I had also heard Hunter croon many times as he went about his daily chores:

> *"Up in the mornin', out on the job, work like a devil for my pay,*
> *But that lucky ole sun's got nothin' to do but roll aroun' heaven all day."*

In retrospect, it's clear that at age five my interpretation of the words to this song was far from their true meaning (I thought *Sun* referred to Jesus the *Son* of God and pictured Him rolling around on heavenly clouds). But, nevertheless, I remember this initial "stage" experience as being extremely exhilarating and found the resulting popularity among my classmates even more rewarding. Both my relishing of this approval by my schoolmates and recognition of my gifts as a performer grew with each of the several school plays to which I was assigned during these early grade years. With each successive role my stuttering speech and shyness were magically and increasingly replaced by a new self-confidence and sense of empowerment. My favorite roles were the fairytale kings and princes which bestowed upon me a sense of the authority and beauty associated with royalty and which also made me the object of considerable female attention which, in turn, made me the envy of the other boys.

This enjoyment and affinity for playacting, however, was in no way connected to any larger, long-term goal. Actually, the primary vocational aspiration which preoccupied me throughout my elementary and high school years was not performing but the visual arts. It all began on the day that my kindergarten sweetheart Lydia Campbell showed me, with unmistakable pride, her big brother's skillful drawing of a deer. I remember being struck by the fine detail in the lifelike penciled depiction. Initially to impress her, I became increasingly determined to prove and improve my own skills at rendering reproductions of just about anything in sight. Five years later, when my fifth-grade teacher, Miss Frank, finally took note of the idle classroom sketches which had been consuming so much of my attention, she not only alerted my family to the special talent she saw in me but, more importantly, suggested that they look into a scholarship being offered to study drawing at the nearby Sachs Department Store next to the elevated train on Third Avenue.

Fortunately, one of the main ingredients of my happy working-class childhood was my family's support and encouragement of my interests and endeavors. This reassuring presence and gentle urging from Mom, Hunter, Nanny, and stepfather Edgar ("Eddie") Queeley to pursue my dreams, whether artistic, athletic, academic, or otherwise, provided the sense of confidence and self-esteem upon which most of my life's successes have been built. So, following Miss Frank's thoughtful suggestion and subsequently spending each Saturday afternoon developing my pastel and charcoal techniques as the youngest member of an advanced drawing class, I was certain that destiny had called me towards a life in the arts. The true and full nature of this calling, I had yet to discover.

Mom married Eddie in 1959, following her short-lived union with Charles Walcott, a man who, despite being a decent provider and hard worker, had a stern and less than amicable disposition, especially with Cookie and me. I remember one particular incident in which Charles, punishing me for some minor (or nonexistent) infraction, locked me in the trunk of his car for the duration of a short family outing. Ultimately, Mom could not tolerate any such behavior which jeopardized the physical and emotional welfare of her children. Despite the inevitable demise of this alliance, however, the relationship did happily result in the birth of my sister Leslie Ann on June 7th, 1956.

Shortly after I'd begun the sixth grade in 1955, we (Mom, Charles, Cookie, and me—Hunter and Nanny followed in 1957) moved from our once multi-ethnic and thriving but now racially isolated and rapidly deteriorating Central Bronx neighborhood to the newly constructed Throgs Neck Public Housing Projects in the far reaches of the Northeast

Bronx. This clean, modern, neatly landscaped development provided another ethnically diverse environment for our family to live in. It encompassed three whole blocks and included ample recreational facilities for the multitude of families that would move in within the first few years after construction. An insular community surrounded by miles of modest-income single and two-family homes, the projects were inhabited by an eclectic mixture of upwardly mobile working-class families which provided me with an abundance of vibrant and attractive personalities to observe and to learn from. Among the large cast of notable neighborhood characters who would influence me during this period were renowned jazz saxophonist Lou Donaldson (whose daughter Lydia was my steady girlfriend during age twelve), the mercurial future poet David Henderson (who would, years later, become one of my literary mentors), and the Caribbean-born, intellectually astute street-corner debater and future political organizer, Courtland Cox.

Several months prior to our moving, Hunter and Nanny had converted from their Methodist faith to Catholicism and at the beginning of that school year transferred Cookie and me (and Aunt Margaret's oldest daughter Lana Gibbons, whom they had adopted) from P.S. 54 to the South Bronx's St. Anthony of Padua Catholic School. Upon our arrival in Throgs Neck a few months later, the three of us were immediately enrolled at the nearly all-white St. Frances de Chantal Elementary School where I was forced to quickly acquire the ability to stand up for myself (both physically and intellectually) and to excel despite the mindless racial prejudice of some of my classmates. It was also here, under the stern, watchful guidance of the school's teaching nuns, that I first discovered a love for poetry, a passion that would sustain and nourish me for a lifetime. The subsequent five-year tour of strict parochial school instruction (three at St. Frances and two at Cardinal Hayes High School, where I enjoyed a brief athletic career as a sprinter on their formidable and highly regarded track squad), proved to be both morally and academically invaluable.

But the regimented Catholic school tradition at Hayes High, in which corporal punishment was not only acceptable but commonplace, became more than I was willing to endure. The day that Brother Cyprius, a diminutive cleric of mixed racial heritage, decided to set an example for his entire class by hauling off and slapping a six-foot-four Irish-American basketball star for some minor infraction ("not paying attention"), I knew that my days at the school were numbered. My transfer from Cardinal Hayes High to Manhattan's High School of Art and Design (A&D) at the start of my junior year proved to be one of the most consequential decisions of my entire youth. Shifting from the rigorously disciplined, all-male, and creatively restrictive environment at Hayes to the coeducational A&D, where artistic expression and liberal thought were encouraged and nurtured, was a watershed experience for me. Within my first few weeks of being there, I virtually exploded with a new-found spirit of exploration and creativity. Furthermore, to have made this transition in 1960, when the entire country was beginning to shift from the conservative, reactionary, and complacent postwar era of Dwight D. Eisenhower to the more socially progressive John F. Kennedy *Camelot* years, could not have been better timed.

My areas of interest and activity at A&D ranged from drawing and painting, with a major in commercial art and advertising illustration (leading to my winning first place in the annual New York Port Authority art contest and a scholarship to the Famous Artists' Correspondence School headed by Norman Rockwell), to theater, where I performed leading roles in all of the school's drama club productions, to speech competition, a field in which I represented my school (with Booker T. Washington's famous "Cast down your buckets" speech) winning second place city-wide, to choral singing, highlighted by a stint with New York's prestigious All-City High School Chorus in my senior year and a performance at Carnegie Hall. All in all, my last two years of high school at A&D provided, by far, my most enjoyable, stimulating, and memorable experiences up to that point.

Then, just prior to my eighteenth birthday (and a few months after the birth of my baby brother Pancho), I found my true calling when I was "discovered" by an accomplished dancer-choreographer, high school physical education instructor, and first-time theater producer named Patricia Taylor Curtis. She and her husband, the gifted composer-musician Norman Curtis, recruited me and others among my 1962 graduating class at A&D to join the cast of their topical musical

Program for IF WE GROW UP with Rick Rotante, 1962.

revue *If We Grow Up*. The irrepressible Ms. Taylor Curtis, who, among other things, had been a dancer and bit player in Otto Preminger's film *Carmen Jones* with Dorothy Dandridge, taught part-time at Art and Design. She had seen me perform in the A&D Spring Festival that year as both a soloist with the school chorus (singing George Gershwin's "Summertime") and as a leading actor in the drama club's festival offering. Upon auditioning me for one of the starring roles in *Grow Up*, the debut production of the newly founded Next Stage Theatre Company, she, along with Norman and their co-producer Gabriel Levinson, not only offered me the part but deemed me a major new talent and began to mentor me in all things related to my development as a burgeoning young performer. Receiving this kind of validation from people as talented and experienced as the Curtises raised my level of self-confidence to unexpected new heights, and the pride that it instilled among my family, especially Hunter, who could now fully invest his early life's dreams within his grandson, only deepened my desire to succeed on this new path.

The Curtises, the first interracial couple I had ever known (she being black and he white), were products of Chicago's progressive community of artist/activists in the tradition of their "Windy City" cohorts and colleagues writer and radio personality Studs Terkel, singer-songwriter Oscar Brown, Jr., director Paul Sills, poet Gwendolyn Brooks, and playwright Lorraine Hansberry. They were also friends with and introduced us to such prominent cultural figures as filmmakers Gordon Parks, Sr., and Gordon Parks, Jr., dance pioneer Alvin Ailey, jazz greats Max Roach and Abbe Lincoln, singer-actress Diahann Carroll and her husband-manager Monte Kay, and theater and nightclub manager Pete Long.

Pete, who had managed Harlem's Apollo Theatre for years, now worked for the D'Lugoff Brothers at their famous Village Gate nightclub on Bleecker Street in Greenwich Village, where he produced a weekly Monday night showcase series to highlight up-and-coming talent. Among the alumni of this prestigious series were Florida jazz musicians Julian "Cannonball" Adderley and his younger brother Nat, a girl singer from Ohio named Nancy Wilson, and two gifted young comedic talents, Flip Wilson and Bill Cosby, who were both promoted to serving as warm-up performers for the club's jazz headliners. Pete invited four cast members, Gil Arieta, Rick Rotante, JoAnne Morgan, and me to perform selections from *If We Grow Up* for several consecutive Monday nights. From my early teens Mom and Eddie had begun introducing me to the sounds of jazz, mainly through the recordings of Miles Davis, Dakota Staton, Gloria Lynn, Jimmy Smith, and others. By age fifteen I was attending the annual jazz concerts at Randall's Island (also produced by Long) where I saw and heard Miles, Trane, and Rollins. Now, at age eighteen, to be singing and dancing at the legendary "Gate" upon the same stage as had many of the music giants of the past twenty years was, for me, an unbelievable, near out-of-body experience. (To my surprise, twelve years later I would meet Pete Long again when hired to play opposite his wife Loretta Long on *Sesame Street.*)

Norman and Patty Curtis inspired their cadre of young protégés, including myself and fellow A&D grads Gil, JoAnne, Rick, Carmen Rivera, Tommy Andrisano, and others to reach for the very best within ourselves, not just for our own personal fulfillment but to contribute towards a better, more humane world. Patty, especially, tried to instill in us an appreciation for the intrinsic relationship between art and society, encouraging a sense of social consciousness as well as an abiding passion for scholarship and excellence in our work.

If We Grow Up, with book, lyrics, direction, and choreography by Patty and music written and performed by Norman, explored such volatile social issues as the Cold War paranoia of the '50s and '60s, the cynicism of Madison Avenue marketing, media-age mediocrity, and the painful effects of racism, all from the perspective of intelligent, informed, and passionate young people. The gravity of these themes, combined with the high energy and optimism that we teenage performers brought to the material, made for a provocative and entertaining theatrical experience. I was featured prominently in several of the show's skits, including *Madison Avenue Macbeth* (in which *Macbeth*'s three "witches" in the guise of male ad executives concoct a deadly brew to seduce and infect the minds of American youth) and *Lovin' and Hatin' Blues* (in which two Southern youths, one black and one white, lament their mandated roles as adversaries). I also did a solo performance of a touching ballad entitled "When Someone Believes in You."

Suddenly, acting and singing, beyond remaining fun for me, became important vehicles in my socio-political education and a viable and highly attractive career choice. *If We Grow Up* received critical acclaim and had more than a year's run in three different Off-Broadway theaters (first the Sheridan Square Playhouse on Seventh Avenue South, then across the street at the Actor's Playhouse, and, finally, at the Rodale Theatre on East 4th Street). The excitement and sense of purpose derived from being part of such an amazing journey was an intoxicating and inspiring experience for all of us. I was flattered by some theater reviewers' comparisons of me to a young Sidney Poitier and was thrilled at being recognized for this debut a few years later by Langston Hughes and Milton Meltzer in their pictorial history of Negro entertainers, *Black Magic*.

Some of us were guided by the Curtises toward professional training to further develop our skills. Gifted songstress JoAnne Morgan and I enrolled at Theodore Mann's Circle in the Square Theater School directly across from the Village Gate on Bleecker Street where we began to study acting with the highly respected young teacher and director (and future head of The Julliard School's theater department) Michael Kahn. For our audition piece we did a scene from Lorraine Hansberry's *A Raisin in the Sun* between Beneatha and her young African suitor Asaiga in which I not only had the task of wooing this "princess of the new world" but also had to adopt a foreign accent. Apparently, Kahn saw some measure of talent in my efforts with the role and in my ability to absorb and then utilize his suggestions to improve upon my performance.

I was instantly intrigued and compelled by the immensity of what I did not know about the craft of acting. Throughout the long run of *Grow Up*, I had worked on the basis of my natural instinct and imagination, tools which could only serve me up to a point. Under Michael's guidance I would begin to explore the more reliable and sustainable techniques of "method" acting. Kahn would leave Circle in the Square within my first several months of enrollment and I continued to study with him after his departure from the school in his own, more advanced workshop at The Writer's Stage on East 4th Street along with fellow students Harvey Keitel, Rufus Collins, Maryanne Schaeffer, Marissa Joffrey, Abigail Rosen, and others. This period of intense scene study with the different combinations of my classmates was an extraordinary time of discovery and growth. The various exercises in relaxation, improvisation, sense memory, and emotional recall to which Michael introduced us allowed me to tap into areas of myself which would open up new levels of creativity within me. My fellow students and I learned how to build a character from the ground up and to utilize our total instrument (our selves) to this end with imagination and skill.

We were all recent apprentices within the thirty-year-old revolution of dramatic theory in America based upon Konstantin Stanislavsky's work with Russia's great Moscow Art Theatre and then later popularized by Elia Kazan and Lee Strasberg with their legendary Actors Studio, the creative laboratory where such luminaries as Marlon Brando, Geraldine Paige, Shelly Winters, Paul Newman, James Dean, and many others had honed their craft. Michael, along with other leading teachers of the day, such as Uta Hagen, Sanford Meisner, Herbert Burghoff, and Bill Hickey, was a gatekeeper to the secrets of this new and undeniably vibrant "school" of acting.

This new American brand of method acting had its critics and naysayers within the world of drama, particularly among the British Shakespearean traditionalists who were trained to focus more upon the external elements of the craft such as speech and movement, but the formulas and exercises which explored and developed the connections between the emotional and psychological life of the actor and that of his character offered a powerful set of tools with which to facilitate the

One of my first professional headshots, 1964. (Courtesy of Frederick Rolf.)

subtle processes of the imagination inherent in all good acting, and within this discipline I slowly began to use these tools to fashion my own creative path. In addition to establishing the fundamental tenets of a solid acting technique, I also began to develop an appreciation of the joys, challenges, and dignity of an acting career and to identify with and align myself within the "fraternity" of my chosen profession.

For nearly two years, while cutting mats and framing pictures at the Artlee Picture Frame Shop in College Point, Queens, I patiently waited to begin my professional theater life in earnest. Along with my roommate and fellow A&D grad (and a supremely gifted painter) Richard Collins, I rented a two-bedroom apartment on Manhattan's Eastside. Finally, on a late spring morning in 1964, I gave my two weeks' notice to Leo Chipkin, my boss and the co-owner of Artlee, explaining that I had been offered an acting job. Leo, whose son Paul had been one of my fellow cast members in *If We Grow Up*, was far from happy and supportive, berating me for "giving up a steady and secure position with a future for the unrealistic dream of becoming an actor." What seemed to upset him even more was the fact that for two years, despite his knowledge of my theatrical ambitions (and unbeknownst to me), he had been grooming me to eventually manage the frame shop for him. Leo's discouragement and seeming lack of appreciation for my ability to succeed in acting (despite his son's well-supported ambitions to pursue a similar career path) triggered a sense of pride and indignation within me and provided me with an extra incentive. I would show him, and everyone else.

Michael had cast me in two summer-stock productions that he was directing at Northport, Long Island's Red Barn Theatre. I was given two roles that were not written as black characters but could easily be assigned "colorblind." First there was *The Fantastiks*, the delightfully upbeat musical a few years into its record-breaking run at Greenwich Village's Sullivan Street Playhouse. I performed the enjoyably challenging but thankless role of The Mute. Omnipresent throughout the play and with no spoken lines, this "invisible" character morphs into wind, rain, snow, leaves, a wall, and other mostly inanimate environmental elements which are essential to the story being told. It provided me with a wonderful exercise in both imagination and physical expression. The next production was Carl Reiner's hilarious autobiographical comedy *Enter Laughing*, in which I played Pike, the stage-manager, a small role mainly comprised of a series of well-timed comic reactions.

For that entire summer I enjoyed the comfortable housing provided for the cast in a lovely bed-and-breakfast inn directly overlooking Long Island's Oyster Bay. The two plays offered me my first chance to act with seasoned veterans such as George Marcy, Ruth Jaroslow, and Frederick Rolf, whose professionalism and competence were a great example for me to study from such close range. Fred Rolf, in particular, was an extremely erudite and versatile character actor, as well as a teacher and director, who took it upon himself to share with me much of his insight and knowledge about the craft over the summer and for many months beyond. Also an experienced portrait photographer, Fred provided me with my first professional head shots to solicit future work. I also had the pleasure that summer of working with and getting to know several other promising newcomers such as Broadway star Tammy Grimes' younger brother Nicholas Grimes, Richard Balin (younger brother to up-and-coming film star Ina Balin), future soap opera actress Kelly Wood, and singer-actor John Davidson, who would soon become a popular television star of the 1960s and '70s (*That's Incredible*).

More significantly, these jobs would initiate my induction into Actors' Equity Association, an important transition for a young professional theater performer. Up to this point I had been limited to working in non-union (and often non-paying) productions, but I was now a full-fledged, rank and file, dues-paying, professional actor. I could and did from this point on begin to make use of the casting information listed in *Backstage* newspaper and *Variety* magazine, as well as from the daily bulletin board listings of the union jobs which were posted at the Equity office in New York's Times Square. Convening regularly with others at this "hangout" for many theater performers, both veterans and novices, was a way of feeling connected to the industry as well as of networking and exchanging inside information.

For about a year prior to this, I had been studying classical singing technique at the Upper Eastside's Manhattan School of Music with vocal coach Cezare Longo, who introduced me to many of the great standards of American popular song by Gershwin, Porter, Ellington, and Berlin. This formal training greatly enhanced the development of my skills as a naturally gifted baritone. Many of the exercises I performed were those used by most classically trained singers. Mr. Longo, an ardent opera buff, tried to instill in me an appreciation for this classical form by taking me to the Metropolitan Opera to see *Der Meistersinger* by Wagner, one of the most arduously long and complicated operas ever written. After watching me suffer through this interminably torturous experience, he admitted that this particular piece was probably not the best choice for my introduction to the art form, an understatement if there ever was one. Although I never developed an affinity for opera, Mr. Longo was able to encourage my innate appreciation for and identification with many of the great "pop" and jazz balladeers of the day, such as Frank Sinatra, Nat "King" Cole, Billy Eckstein, Sammy Davis, Jr., Tony Bennett, and Joe Williams.

During this same period I continued my dance training with classes at the Alvin Ailey Dance Theater. The choreography in *If We Grow Up* had been my introduction to modern interpretive dance and Patty Curtis had offered additional instruction to most of the Next Stage members. I had always loved to dance and was inspired by watching Hunter and Nanny demonstrate their ballroom or soft-shoe prowess, but I found this new level of formal discipline to be both challenging and exhilarating. Now, two or three times a week I dutifully reported to City Center on Eighth Avenue where I would submit my body to the grueling modern dance routines being taught by Patty's friend and colleague Thelma Hill.

These disciplines, both vocal and physical, would serve me well over the years in my work as an actor. They were especially useful in my first several jobs as an Equity member, primarily in musical productions which required a combination of singing, dancing, and acting skills. Shows such as the Next Stage Theatre's second production, *Unfinished Business* (which also provided me with my first television experience on CBS-TV's *Repertory Workshop*); the Harnick-Adams musical productions of *Young Mark Twain* and *Young Tom Jefferson*, which were performed for schoolchildren around the boroughs of New York City; an Off-Broadway version of Rodgers and Hammerstein's *South Pacific* with Gordon Watkins in which I played one of the show's singing and dancing sailors ("There Is Nothing Like a Dame"); and the Thirteenth Street Theatre productions of *Epilogue* and *Smarty Party* all allowed me to develop my performing skills while also earning a modest income (the Equity minimum salary of $60/per week).

In addition to formal study and professional experience, an equally important part of my education was in absorbing some of the very best theater, dance, and music that New York City had to offer during the early sixties. Greenwich Village was the primary breeding ground for many of the major cutting-edge artists in jazz, blues, and folk music, as well as stand-up comedy and theater. Most Broadway theater was still both substantive and affordable, and I had the privilege of seeing some of the period's most celebrated productions, among the more famous being Edward Albee's *Who's Afraid of Virginia Woolf?* with Uta Hagen and Arthur Hill. I also had the pleasure of seeing Lee Strasberg's now legendary Actors Studio productions of Anton Chekhov's *Three Sisters* and Eugene O'Neill's *Strange Interlude* (which ran for over four hours and included a break for dinner). Both plays starred the incomparable Geraldine Paige, whose mercurial presence was a wonder to behold, and featured other stellar Studio members such as Kim Stanley, Pat Hingle, Rip Torn, and James Olson.

I was also mesmerized by the inspired comedic work of the young Alan Arkin in *Enter Laughing*, and of Peter Cook, Jonathan Miller, and

Dudley Moore in the hit British import *Beyond the Fringe*. I was deeply impressed by the electrifying performance of Clarence Williams III in *Slow Dance on the Killing Ground* and even more so by Alec Guinness's spellbinding portrayal of Welsh poet Dylan Thomas in *Dylan*. At one point in the play, Guinness lay prone near the edge of the stage and, in his mellifluous, dulcet-toned voice, recited one of Thomas's lyrical masterpieces. I became utterly awestruck as the relaxed, almost nonchalant ease with which this great actor had cast his hypnotic spell over the entire audience provoked a most delicious mixture of envy and admiration within me and a burning desire to do the same.

Further downtown below 14th Street in the East and West Village was the exciting world of Off-Broadway theater which had only begun to emerge within the prior decade. With smaller houses, lower salaries, and cheaper tickets, Off-Broadway offered edgier, more experimental and challenging fare for audiences to absorb. I was fortunate enough during that period to have seen such gems as Ulu Grosbard's production of the riveting Arthur Miller play *A View from the Bridge* at the Sheridan Square Playhouse, which included standout work by Robert Duvall as Eddie Carbone and by Jon Voight as Rodolfo, his young Italian immigrant cousin (I found out later that the stage manager for this production had been a struggling young actor named Dustin Hoffman) and my acting teacher Michael Kahn's production of Adrienne Kennedy's haunting play *Funnyhouse of a Negro,* which featured a startling tour-de-force performance by Billie Allen as well as solid work from Ellen Holly, Cynthia Belgrave, and Norman Bush.

Among the most provocative and stimulating plays that I observed during this period were the three landmark early offerings from LeRoi Jones (later known as Amiri Baraka). Jones was on the verge of redefining the role and the parameters of expression among black theater artists and, in the process, sending shockwaves through New York's theatrical establishment. First there was the double-billed presentation at St. Mark's Playhouse of *The Toilet* with D'urville Martin, Gary Bolling, Antonio Fargas, Jaime Sanchez, and Rony Clanton, and *The Slave,* featuring Al Freeman, Jr. Soon after that came the Cherry Lane Theatre's production of *The Dutchman* with Robert "Bobby Dean" Hooks. In *The*

Dutchman Jones gave eloquent voice to the anger and frustration of my own emerging generation of blacks. In workshop sessions with Michael, I had the opportunity to study and perform the role of Clay in this piece. Young, educated, articulate, and acutely aware of the contradictions within white society, Jones' character offered me one of my most powerful early experiences of self-discovery through acting.

My exposure to such high-quality work during these early years was an important supplement to the development of my own skills. As a young student of the craft, I was especially impressed and informed by the well-seasoned and rotating ensemble cast of black actors in the famously long-running, provocative, and ground-breaking production of Jean Genet's *The Blacks*. Ironically, this play, which had been written by a white French sociopath, would become a cornerstone in the history of black theater and provide a turning point for the sensibilities of the new generation of black theater artists during this time of confrontational social activism in America.

Running at The St. Mark's Playhouse in the East Village for nearly four years, *The Blacks* became my introduction to the work of such actors as Roscoe Lee Browne, James Earl Jones, Louis Gossett Jr., Thelma Oliver, Ethel Ayler, Helen Martin, Godfrey Cambridge, Moses Gunn, Esther Rolle, Cicely Tyson, Louise Stubbs, Lex Monson, Nichelle Nichols, Vinie Burrows, Lincoln Kilpatrick, Raymond St. Jacque, Maya Angelou, Clebert Ford, Roxie Roker, Harold Scott, and others whose professional and social circle would gather regularly at the Lower East Side's Orchidia Bar and Restaurant. This large extended family of artists became my new heroes and the world which they inhabited became a fascinating new breeding ground and a well of knowledge from which I and other young thespians could continuously draw inspiration.

A brief "golden" age of Off- and Off-Off-Broadway production during this period provided many of these and other performers (both black and white) with a steady flow of employment in a variety of plays, many of them avant-garde and artistically challenging. James Earl Jones, Cicely Tyson, and Lou Gossett, in particular, seemed to each be in a new play every few weeks. Over the intervening years, some of these people (Jones, Tyson, Gossett, Angelou, Nichols, etc.) would become household names. In those early years, however, as I and others like Roger Robinson, D'urville Martin, Gary Bolling, Yvette Hawkins, Norman Bush, Tony Fargas, and Hattie Winston attempted to gain a foothold within the New York theater world, these men and women, as accessible African-American practitioners of theater craft, would serve as important and influential role models for us in the pursuit of our new profession. The power of their examples inspired us with the courage to believe in our own abilities to succeed.

CHAPTER TWO

Southern Journey

Desire

Driving down slinky New Orleans
Turns me on
And makes me sad.
Out in Desire
Where the Jazz City funk floats
Over the street holes
And grooves above the ditches
That stifle black domestics
And greasy high-conked cats
Screaming
Jumping up and down in their own sweat.
It turns me on
And makes me sad.
Out in Desire
All beauty in chains
Rumbling deep somewhere-between-the-stomach-and-the-
 brain.
Oh the day will come
Out in Desire
The day will come

7/65

In the early sixties, under the sway of the politically astute and vastly more experienced personalities of the Curtises and their colleagues, my peers and I were prime candidates for recruitment into the ranks of the progressive social movements of our day. The spirit of dedication and optimism during the Kennedy White House years which had been preceded by the highly publicized civil rights successes in Montgomery, Birmingham, and Little Rock still energized our generation, having yet to be transformed by the series of assassinations and urban uprisings which would come to characterize the end of this tumultuous decade. And so, after a few years of studying and pounding the streets of Manhattan as a card-carrying Equity member, and landing the occasional Off-Off-Broadway or touring gig, I found myself in 1965, at the tender age of twenty-one, touring the South with The Free Southern Theater (FST), the politically and morally galvanizing theatrical wing of the student civil rights movement.

This geographically and racially diverse group of thespians, founded in 1964 by two young black freedom workers, Illinois native John O'Neal and Gilbert Moses of Cleveland, Ohio, had first caught my attention in early '65 when the highly regarded jazz songwriter-singer Oscar Brown, Jr., showed me a *Village Voice* article which described their initial season. At the time I was featured with Oscar and his wife Jean Pace in a production of his entitled *The Worlds of Oscar Brown, Jr.* at New York's Gramercy Arts Theatre in which I sang two solos, "World Full of Gray" and "Opportunity Please Knock." About a year prior to this, I had gone to see Oscar perform at the Cafe Au Go Go in Greenwich Village. During intermission I took the opportunity to go backstage and introduce myself to him as a friend and protégé of his fellow Chicago natives Norman and Patty Curtis. Like the star-struck twenty-year-old that I was, I told Brown how much I admired his work, having been thoroughly captivated by his two groundbreaking albums of the early '60s, *Sin and Soul* and *Between Heaven and Hell*, which featured such classic songs as "Brown Baby," "Dat Dere," "Signifyin' Monkey," "Work Song," and "But I Was Cool." I told him that Norman, who had co-written "Rags and Old Iron" and other compositions with him, had taught me these as well as several lesser known songs of his. During the second half of his set, to my utter surprise, Oscar introduced me to the audience and asked that I come to the stage and perform one of my favorite selections from *Between Heaven and Hell*, the coming-of-age ballad "World Full of Gray."

"*When I was a lad, simple notions I had.*
There was wrong, here was right, it was plain black and white.
But now that I'm grown, in the world on my own,
The scenes I survey show nothing but gray...."

Evidently, I did okay. Now, a year later, as a trusted colleague and mentor, Oscar encouraged my interest in FST and proved instrumental

Applauding Dr. King at historic March on Washington with Paul Chipkin and his mom, Ruth, 1963. (Courtesy of Leo Chipkin.)

in my decision to join them. But it was the sheer bravery and physical defiance of this young troupe that had truly captured my imagination. Throughout and since my high school years I had followed the exploits of the courageous young Freedom Riders and sit-in protesters of the movement (one of whom I had portrayed in *If We Grow Up*) as they risked their lives in the fight for freedom and justice. Personally, I had been deeply moved by the experience of attending, with the family of fellow Next Stage Theatre member Paul Chipkin (Leo's son), the historic 1963 March on Washington. I remember being totally transfixed as Martin Luther King, Jr., delivered his famous "*I Have a Dream*" speech. For many in attendance that day, including myself, this was our first experience with direct civil rights action. But for the scores of movement veterans who were also present, this was the culmination of months and years of selfless commitment to the cause of social justice. These people had earned the respect and admiration of much of the nation, and I felt personally challenged by their example to play a more meaningful role in this momentous effort. The Free Southern Theater presented me with a chance to do just that.

Upon my first meeting with FST co-founder John O'Neal in New York, I was initially struck by the combination of youth and maturity in his manner and gaze and, even more importantly, by his sincerity. John was a graduate of Carbondale's University of Southern Illinois who had first gone south as a member of the Student Non-violent Coordinating Committee (SNCC). I found his obvious intelligence, compassion, and total commitment to the movement completely infectious and his laid-back, unassuming, and contemplative style disarming. Right away, I knew that FST was the place for me. The Free Southern Theater seemed to embody the essence of what I saw as a moral and social imperative within the theatrical community at that time as well as within the nation. Its philosophy of inclusion, reflected in its bi-racial membership and its multi-cultural repertoire, mirrored the politics of the mainstream movement of the day. Not surprisingly, the company had the support of some of the country's most prominent cultural figures, including Harry Belafonte, Bob Dylan, Ruby Dee, Ossie Davis, Gene Kelly, James Baldwin, Langston Hughes, Henry Fonda, Sidney Poitier, and Dorothy Dandridge, to name a few. By joining FST, I would be making a personal contribution to the struggle at a pivotal time in our history in as dramatic a fashion as I could imagine. For me, no better *opportunity* existed.

On my initial trip south, while waiting to change planes in Atlanta, I had an unforgettable encounter and brief conversation with Dr. Martin Luther King, Jr. His entry into the waiting area caused quite a stir among the nearly all white collection of passengers there, and when he approached me, extending his hand to shake mine, in addition to being utterly dumbstruck, I felt a wonderful sense of pride and humility. He was at the airport waiting for his friend and ally Harry Belafonte who, when he arrived, was mistaken by most of my fellow travelers for another famous person. "Well, I'll be danged if it ain't Cassius Clay," as one said. I realized, much later, that King and Belafonte were in the planning stages for the pivotal march across Selma, Alabama's Edmund Pettus Bridge.

What impressed me most about Dr. King, besides the warm sincerity of his greeting, was the powerful sense of compassion and dignity which he exuded with an effortless charm, much like what I would observe, a few years later in a brief encounter with boxing's "greatest" Muhammad Ali. This fortuitous meeting with Martin was surely a benediction to my ensuing journey. It was also a precursor to my acquaintance, during the next two years, with other influential figures within the civil rights movement, including Julian Bond, James Bevel, Stokely Carmichael, James Forman, and Andrew Young. I would also have a most surprising reunion with former Bronx neighborhood mentor and role model and now SNCC field coordinator Courtland Cox (who was, I believe, as surprised to see me in this new context as I was to see him).

When I arrived in New Orleans, the new home of FST after having spent its first year based in Jackson, Mississippi, I was met at the airport by Gilbert Moses and his wife, Detroit native Denise Nicholas. Gilbert, a recent graduate of Ohio's Oberlin College who wore wire-rimmed glasses and a wild, thick mane of hair, had the intensity, intelligence, and charisma of a natural-born leader and innovator. Denise, who had come south directly from the University of Michigan at Ann Arbor, was equally intelligent and had the luminescent, copper-toned beauty and bearing of a young princess. These two people would have a major impact on my life and work over the next decade. For starters, they and the FST would introduce me to both the philosophy and the actuality of a "revolutionary-collective" lifestyle in which all company members were equally compensated with the barest of minimums ($35.00 a week, at best; even in 1965 this was a minuscule sum to live on). In a remote and relatively rundown section of the city, the theater's new headquarters was in an old abandoned building, ironically known as the Pentagon. It included ample office space and a huge area for rehearsals and workshops but contained no performance facility (FST was, after all, a touring company).

Not too surprisingly, a high percentage of those who came to join FST in the early weeks of this, its second season, would leave within the first month, having been totally unprepared for the physical and emotional rigors of "guerrilla" theater. In fact, most of these transient recruits, young, white, and middle class, were well-meaning northern liberals who had come south with the intention of volunteering a summer vacation from their "real" lives to offer whatever assistance they could to this worthy cause. Although some would prove to be extraordinarily committed, ultimately, most of them were not in it for the long haul.

Personally, I found myself on excitingly new and remarkably fertile ground with FST. Coming from a New York theatrical background with Equity affiliation, as had fellow New Yorker Murray Levy, South Carolina native Emalyn Hawkins, Circle in the Square classmate Marissa Joffrey, and Buffalo native Robert "Big Daddy" Costley, I was afforded a level of professional respect which I had never encountered before. Costley, a forty-something divorcé who would go on to spend the remaining twenty-five years of his life in New Orleans, had brought a lifetime of experience with him to this "brave new adventure." Big Daddy, as the nickname implies, was a bear of a man with a mixed gray goatee who walked with a slightly bent posture due to a permanent spinal condition for which I didn't know the name. The father of an undetermined number of offspring, he endearingly referred to all of us twenty-somethings as his "chillun" and was especially laudatory in his evaluation of my talents as an actor, singer, and dancer, enhancing my already healthy measure of self-confidence. Indeed, the rigorous training and apprenticeship of the previous three years had prepared me well for this new challenge.

My induction into the Free Southern Theater became a crash course in both the political and social realities of the Deep South. The Southern "Jim Crow" laws and the reign of terror they protected were, as everyone knew, the main set of conditions against which the civil rights struggle was being fought. Being in the South caused a series of culture shocks and instantly raised the level of political awareness among all of us newly transported non-Southerners, both black and white.

My rude initiation into Southern realities occurred early one day after just moving into my first apartment in New Orleans' French Quarter along with my roommate Murray Levy, a twenty-eight-year-old Queens native and Broadway, Off-Broadway, and one-year FST veteran. We had help from two of my fellow newcomers, Robert Cordier, a burly, curly-headed Belgian theater director in his early thirties, and the company's new technical director David McLaughlin, the twenty-two-year-old son of a Massachusetts judge who had made the long trip from New England to New Orleans astride his Harley Davidson motorcycle, a feat which automatically raised him and his arrival to heroic status within the group.

After moving Murray's and my meager belongings into our second-story flat, the four of us decided to celebrate over a few beers. Our bodies slightly fatigued from labor, we sauntered unassumingly into the local neighborhood pub right down the block from the apartment house. We perched ourselves on the vinyl-covered stools at the bar for several minutes trying, unsuccessfully, to attract the barmaid's attention. Finally, she approached us with a terse "I cain't serve y'all." Our request for service had not only been denied but, to our great surprise, within just a few minutes, was also met by a full squadron from the New Orleans Police Department, which had literally surrounded the bar. My three white friends and I, who had stumbled unintentionally into this sit-in protest, were each handcuffed, charged with violating the archaic "vagrancy" laws (a common ploy used to detain civil rights workers), then carted off to spend that day in one of the Crescent City's segregated jailhouses.

I didn't know where the others had been taken, but I was detained for several hours in a cubicle with the dimensions of an average size bathroom along with about ten to fifteen other mostly young black men who were being held on undetermined charges. Eventually I was brought upstairs where, during an unnecessarily rough finger-printing session, two of New Orleans' "finest" attacked me with the most vicious barrage of obscenities and racial epithets I'd ever heard. With one holding me in an arm lock from behind and the other forcefully jamming my fingers into the ink blotter and printing cards, they both taunted, "I bet you like bein' aroun' them white gals, eh, Sambo? Come down here from up no'th ta get some o' that white poontang, huh, nigger? Goddammit, who in the hell you think you are, boy?" My heart filled with rage, and the effort to contain it was all consuming. For the first time in my life, I felt the vengeful urge to kill another human being, a kind of impulse which my straight and narrow Catholic upbringing had successfully taught me to suppress. In just that instant, however, the indignity and pain of America's legacy of slavery and racism had hit my gut like a jackhammer, igniting the fires of outrage within me as never before and fueling my determination for the battles that lay ahead. Suddenly, I was also forced to appreciate how difficult in practice was the philosophy of non-violent resistance and of "loving one's enemy" to which Dr. King and his followers were so deeply committed.

Back home in New York writer James Baldwin and other supporters were already using the news media to express their outrage at our arrests. By early evening, our local American Civil Liberties Union (ACLU) legal team had arranged to have us released on bail. It was soon decided that our case would be used to contest the constitutionality of the city's vagrancy laws. This decision, to no one's surprise, led to the swift dismissal of all charges.

One afternoon a few weeks later I was pulled over by patrol officers while riding my bicycle and arrested for going the wrong way on a one-way street. With satisfied smirks on their faces, the officers calmly followed me back to my apartment where I was allowed to deposit my bike, after which I was unceremoniously escorted to the precinct. After being held for a few hours, I paid the thirty-dollar fine (five dollars short of a week's salary) and was released. These and other attempts by the police to intimidate me and my colleagues only helped to solidify our resolve and strengthen our commitment to the civil rights struggle.

Another experience during my early months with FST further added to my personal and political evolution. Not too long after having settled into my new residence, I was contacted by the recruitment office of the United States Armed Forces and told to report to the local draft board for my induction examination. I was shocked and mortified. Despite my father's "casualties," I had grown up with the typical boyhood sense of glory and heroism attached to armed service, with every intention of eventually serving my country, as had my father, stepfather, uncles, and grandfathers before me. This greeting, however, could not have come at a worse time. In 1965 the Lyndon Johnson administration was continuing to escalate America's so-called "police action" in Southeast Asia into a full-scale military campaign. Antiwar protests had already begun and were now growing into a national movement. Some of the civil rights leaders, most notably Stokely Carmichael of SNCC and Dr. King of the Southern Christian Leadership Conference (SCLC), were speaking out on the issue. Those of us in the struggle were keenly aware of the morally bankrupt global rationales and the futility inherent in this conflict.

Beyond being conscientiously opposed to the Vietnam war, I had already enlisted in the army of my choice. Albeit non-violently, I was serving on the front lines of a civil rights war being waged on the homefront. John O'Neal had already filed for "conscientious objector" status and was in the midst of what would become a prolonged legal battle. Unlike John, however, I did not have a degree in philosophy, nor was I prepared to spend years in and out of court to achieve an uncertain end. As far as my friends and I were concerned, there was little doubt that my classification would be 1A. I was in excellent health with no physical impairments and knew that unless I did something to prevent it I would soon find myself in the jungles of Vietnam with a mission to kill. As the dreaded day of reckoning approached, the question was not "if" but "how" I would avoid induction. With the fervent moral support and encouragement of my new colleagues, as well as from my family back home, I walked through the doors of the draft board office determined to employ whatever means necessary to convince Uncle Sam that I was an unfit candidate for service.

Fortunately for me, the young psychologist to whom I was sent after admitting, in writing, to several of types of deviance, including bedwetting and homosexuality, was even wetter behind the ears than I was. Through sheer acting talent and inspired virtuoso storytelling, I was able to convince this new Ph.D. that I had severe psychological issues which needed serious attention and "unfortunately" disqualified me from service in the military. Before leaving, I assured him that I would seek the professional counseling I so needed and also "come out" to my family back home and re-establish with them a "relationship built upon honesty and integrity."

A few weeks later, upon receiving notification of my 4F status in the mail, I rejoiced and celebrated with my friends into the wee hours. Although initially somewhat uncomfortable about having lied and not having had the moral and intellectual fortitude to pursue the more "honorable" course of John O'Neal or let alone the history-making journey of Muhammad Ali, I soon came to feel that my decision was, undoubtedly, the right one for me. In spite of my respect and enormous sympathy for those who did go to Vietnam, I have certainly never regretted not going. More importantly, I would continue to play a part in my momentous chosen task alongside a group of people whom I was already coming to love as well as respect.

I found that the South, and New Orleans in particular with its sultry climate and hybrid cultural mix, had awakened within me new levels of creativity as well as a deeper sense of national history which, until then, had been mostly academic. Walking along the cobblestone streets of the French Quarter in this mythic "Jazz City," I could easily imagine myself in an earlier, far less familiar time. The great musical legacy which continued to thrive and expand, the architecture, the food, the native Creole dialect, all combined to evoke a spiritual connection to an ancestral past still living within the people of New Orleans. This sense of

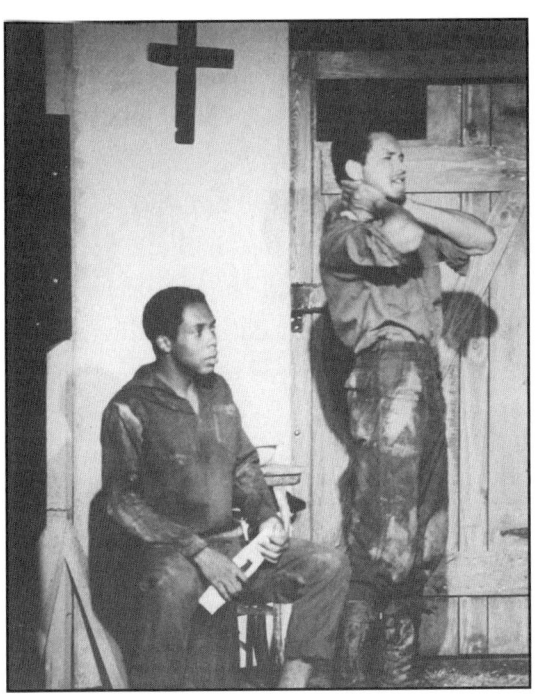

Scene from THE RIFLES OF SENORA CARRAR with Gilbert Moses, 1965. (Courtesy of John O'Neal and Free Southern Theater Archives.)

historical relevance became integral to our work on such plays as Martin Duberman's *In White America*, Bertolt Brecht's *The Rifles of Senora Carrar*, and Sean O'Casey's *Shadow of a Gunman*, infusing into each of them a vitality which we all found to be absolutely electrifying.

In addition to the rich cultural traditions of New Orleans and of the South in general, I also became exposed to some of the new civil rights–influenced forms of expression that, along with the work of FST, were becoming emblematic of the struggle for freedom that was being waged throughout the South. The Freedom Singers were a small a cappella group of vocalists headed by Cordell and Bernice Johnson Reagon that had emerged from within the ranks of SNCC, as had the FST itself. Their spirited and harmonic renditions of songs that were rooted in the black church but reworded with lyrics of protest quickly became the anthems of the movement. Songs such as "We Shall Not Be Moved," "Wade in the Water," "Oh Freedom," and the now world-renowned "We Shall Overcome" were standards known to all within the struggle. During my second year with FST I became acquainted with a New York–based band of performing artists headed by Mark Primus and Norman Jacob when we hosted the New Orleans leg of their southern tour. Known as the Afro-American Folkloric Troupe, they performed a blend of original and traditional material, including songs, poems, and tales of protest.

During my initial season in '65 the FST toured throughout the most racist and politically repressive of the southern states: Louisiana, Georgia, Alabama, and Mississippi. For our mostly rural black audiences the themes of resistance to injustice within the plays we performed took on new meaning and a sense of urgency, often paralleling the current events of their lives and unleashing a sense of power that resonated within us all. By the middle of my first of two seasons with FST, we had developed into a highly motivated ensemble. This cohesiveness was best exemplified during our visits that year to Jonesboro and Bogalusa, Louisiana, which we all knew as the homes of Charles Simms, A.Z. Young, and their famous Deacons for Defense and Justice. This small but militant band of mature black men, who had inspired a new stance of self-defense among many of the younger generation of blacks, notably the Black Panthers and SNCC, served as our personal bodyguards and escorts during our stay.

Unknown to us, news of our pending visits had inspired threats from the local Ku Klux Klan. Late during the night of our arrival in Jonesboro three of our company members, two whites, Robert Cordier and Billy Zukof, and one black, Joe Perry, found some food at an after-hours joint near our housing. On the way back they were pulled over by the local police and taken to the station house where they were harassed and threatened and eventually released, on foot. The police then alerted the Klan that two "nigger lovers and a nigger were loose" and to "pick them up." Joe, Billy, and Robert spent the next three terrifying hours eluding the cops and the Klansmen in the thick Louisiana woods until Billy secretly entered a house and used the phone. One of the Deacons immediately came to where they were, picked them up, and brought them safely "home."

We had come to northern Louisiana intending simply to perform that season's repertoire, but the impact that this incident and the strength of these two communities had upon us as a group of artists transformed us, and we were moved to alter our agenda. Instead of just presenting the works of Duberman and Brecht to our hosts, under Gilbert's inspired direction, we proceeded to mount two original semi-improvisational productions, *The Jonesboro Story* and *The Bogalusa Story*, which would tell the specific and immensely heroic tales of these communities in their struggles against the terrors of racism. Through the Deacons we arranged for meetings with some of the key players in recent confrontational episodes between the white and black communities. Together we re-created, sometimes verbatim, the incidents described, with our white company members portraying the local whites, our black actors performing the larger, more demanding roles of the movement's leaders and protagonists, and in many cases using some of the actual participants from the events to further dramatize our story. A young female Jonesboro native by the name of Bessie Dill, blessed with a powerful presence and a wondrous singing voice, stole the show with her renditions of some of the movement's great freedom songs. It was almost as if she had been waiting her whole life for this, her moment to shine on stage.

These "plays" still rank among the most thrilling and edifying experiences of my life in the theater. Almost magically, actors and audience had truthfully and viscerally become one, obliterating the lines between life and art. For us actors, being on stage and performing alongside

Rehearsing IN WHITE AMERICA with Denise Nicholas and Robert "Big Daddy" Costley, 1965. (Courtesy of John O'Neal and Free Southern Theater Archives.)

some of the heroes whose lives we were depicting was a truly indelible experience. Although these were far from the most artistically polished productions within our repertoire, they unquestionably represented the spirit of FST at its best.

Certainly one of the most fundamental components of FST's success was the theater's relationship to its audience. During this period in the South, a racially integrated company such as ours, by necessity, took refuge and comfort in the hospitality of the black communities among which we moved and performed. There were virtually no hotels willing to accommodate us even if we could afford to pay for rooms, which we could not. Instead, a company member (usually John) would precede us. Through a network of churches and civil rights groups, he would arrange for housing and food to sustain us during our visit. In many instances, the church itself would serve as our theater. At other times, we would perform in community centers, schools, or in open fields. I especially enjoyed when we were hosted by some of the region's colleges and universities, including Tuskegee, Tulane, Dillard, Tougaloo, and Morehouse, and performed on campus for the students and faculty.

Our first such visit was to Tougaloo in Mississippi where we spent a week researching the historical context of our roles in *In White America* by visiting old plantations and other sites of the pre–Civil War Confederacy. During our stays at Alabama's Tuskegee Institute and Georgia's Morehouse College one could readily sense the traditions of black progress and self-improvement that were the legacies of their famous founders and alumni. Performing at New Orleans' own Dillard University and the predominately white Tulane University, where some faculty members had become close friends and colleagues of FST, felt very much to us like being at home. These opportunities had also allowed me to feel a part of, if only fleetingly, the sequestered world of higher education which I had not had the privilege of fully experiencing firsthand.

The financial contributions made by these and other institutions as well as those from foundation grants and individual donors provided the money to run FST. Since a substantial portion of our general audience was unable to pay even a minimal amount, although donations were accepted, as a matter of policy admission to all performances was free of charge. Without the moral support and generosity, not to mention the courage, of the plain small-town Southern folk who served as our hosts, FST could never have survived as it did.

This initial year with FST was also highlighted by my first serious attempts at writing. I studied under the expert tutelage of poet, essayist, and New Orleans native Tom Dent. Tom was son to the president of Dillard University and a childhood friend and lifelong confidant of Andrew Young, the esteemed civil-rights leader and future congressman, UN ambassador, and Atlanta mayor. After spending a number of years both in New York City and abroad, working as a writer, editor (*Umbra Magazine*), and political activist, Tom returned to the city of his birth in 1965, well-schooled, knowledgeable, and accomplished. The civil rights movement, and FST in particular, gave him a reason to come back home. He became a friend and mentor to us, sharing generously of his time and wisdom and offering workshops to those of us who were interested in writing. Finally, the love for poetry which had been planted within me ten years earlier by the nuns at St. Frances School found the necessary guidance and encouragement to take shape and test its wings. In addition to his role as teacher, Tom also provided administrative leadership throughout the theater's remaining years.

My second season with FST, in 1966, was characterized most strongly by the new "Black consciousness" and sense of militancy which had been generated, to a large extent, by Malcolm X's earthshaking collaboration with Alex Haley, *The Autobiography of Malcolm X*, as well as by Stokely Carmichael's highly publicized call for "Black Power" and by the founding of the Black Panther Party in Oakland, California. These milestones caused considerable debate and consternation within the ranks of not only our company but throughout the movement and beyond. These events and this period also marked a coming of age for many, both black and white, forcing us all to consider and reconsider some of the deeper implications inherent in the struggle for "liberation" and in the psychological influences of America's racial legacy. Like many other Northerners of my generation, I had had a racially diverse educational experience, establishing friendships with whites of various ethnicities, as well as with blacks, Hispanics, and Asians. The emergence of this new separatism within the struggle, which would foster the birth of the Black cultural revolution of the 1970s, seemed at first, in the eyes of many, to contradict the very value system upon which the movement had been founded. Motivated by the idealism of a racially integrated struggle, we had brought together people of goodwill, both black and white, to combat the evils of bigotry and oppression. To most of our generation and certainly among our elders, this represented the best hope for America's future.

As was true of other organizations within the movement, however, the membership within FST in 1966, in spite of its being founded and directed by African-Americans, was in fact overwhelmingly white. Spearheaded mostly by the desire among Gilbert, Denise, and myself for a theater that spoke primarily from a black cultural viewpoint, the soul searching and ensuing debates around this issue took their toll upon our company. Among the results of this debate was the redefinition of the Free Southern Theater as a "Black" theater, one that would, for the most part, be produced by and about black people. A few whites stayed on as company members, including Murray, newly arrived technical director Erik Lewis of New York, and Tulane University professor, *Drama Review* editor, and theater advisor Richard Schechner. The continued inclusion of these three talented and dedicated individuals ranked among the year's more well advised and judicious decisions. Despite the new cultural emphasis, it represented, as did countless other examples throughout the history of progressive activism in America, the successful collaboration between blacks and Jews in the struggle for social justice. But a sea change had clearly occurred within the freedom movement and within the country at large, and a new spirit of black self-determination and cultural awareness had begun to take hold among my generation.

One of the offshoots of this new awareness was our decision to move the theater's headquarters from the more neutrally located Pentagon building to the heart of the most culturally and economically deprived area of New Orleans, Desire. Immortalized by Tennessee Williams' legendary 1940s drama *A Streetcar Named Desire*, this severely blighted section of the city had long since ceased to be served by the famous streetcar or most other public facilities. Our new building, which had previously been used as a small food market, quickly became a center of interest and activity for many in the community, particularly its young residents. This led to my first attempts at both teaching and directing. I began a community acting workshop to develop young talent. Prior to this, just weeks before the season was to have started and to everyone's surprise, Gilbert suddenly left the company for what he described as personal and philosophical reasons. I was asked by John and Tom to assume the role of FST's artistic director, which I did, reluctantly. This was not a position that I had envisioned or sought for myself but one that I did feel obligated to perform for the sake of the theater's survival. Fortunately, I had the loyalty and support of the entire company, which helped to turn this sudden and unexpected challenge into an invaluable learning experience for me. Also, and to my great benefit, FST would turn out to be only the first of several collaborations I would have with Gilbert Moses, certainly one of the most immensely gifted individuals that I have ever known (see Chapters four and seven).

Meanwhile, the repertoire of FST's 1966 touring season, as performed by Georgia native Joe Perry, New Orleans workshop protégé Sam Hill, Big Daddy, Murray, Denise, and myself, consisted of the originally compiled *An Evening of African and Afro-American Poetry* (I was thrilled to include my own poem "Desire"), *Does Man Help Man?* by Bertolt Brecht, *I Speak of Africa*, a play with masks by William Plomer (my directing debut), and a new play which had been written by Gilbert, entitled *Roots*, ably directed by Murray and performed by Denise and myself, which explored the relationship of an elderly Southern couple. Because of both the two-character format and the characters' advanced age, the part of "Ray" in this play proved to be, by far, the most ambitious and rewarding in my tenure with FST.

Overall, my two years with the Free Southern Theater were among the most challenging, tumultuous, exhilarating, exhausting, romantic, infuriating, and absolutely indelible of my life. To know that I contributed a part of my early career's work to such a noble and historic effort has brought me increasing pride over the years. With the cultural, social, and political movements of the sixties having had such an enormous impact on what America has since become, for many of my generation the extent of our participation in these struggles has come to define a large part of who we are. The influence of my fellow participants in this courageous enterprise, such as John, Gilbert, Denise, Murray, Tom, Big Daddy, and others, is still felt by me four decades later. Also, the many dedicated foot soldiers of the movement with whom I became friendly during this time, including Rudy Lombard, Jerome Smith, Oretha Castle, Matt "Flukie" Suarez, Lolis Elie, Charlie Cobb, Ruth Howard, and Donna Moses, were powerful role models and living symbols of social conscience in action for me and others to emulate.

But the most abiding and meaningful impressions that I took away from my two seasons with FST were of the many unsung heroes whose dignity and courage in the face of overwhelming brutality stand as glorious testimony to the basic decency of mankind. During those two years I had become deeply affected by the hospitality, humility, and heroism of the citizens of Atlanta, Georgia; of Selma and Tuskegee, Alabama; of Bogalusa, Jonesboro, and New Orleans, Louisiana; and of McComb, Vicksburg, Hattiesburg, Greenwood, Laurel, Jackson, Natchez, Kilmichael, Grenada, Edwards, and Sunflower, Mississippi; which rekindled within me an appreciation of the transcendent beauty and power of the human spirit. My time with the Free Southern Theater was a period of enormous growth as an artist and, more importantly, as a man. The lessons which I learned during this "Southern journey" about selfless commitment to a higher cause, resiliency, and the ability to adapt to change, and the rewards of group camaraderie would serve me well in the "graduate" work that lay just ahead.

Portrait by Toby Macbeth, 1972.

CHAPTER THREE
THE PRODIGAL SON RETURNS

Harlem Stew

In this midsummer
The nights are hung with the musk
Of people being lovers and gamblers
Fadin' 'gainst the stoops
With intermittent waves of chicken smells
                      and rib smells
                      and food smells
And the funk of bodies being soul bearers
                      movin' in the grooves
                      of tenement canyons
In these July days and nights
The city tribes
Wallow in the life of thick dreams
Being smothered in wet heat
And nourished by heavy laden women
Flaunting their succulence
                      to the journeyer who
                      resides within
Within this sphere
Where weary wine drinkers
Weigh their wills against their woes
And husky tones are sung
                      in friendly beckoning
While melodies are wrung
                      from a needle's deadly sting
Simmering in this evening brew
                      is a lonely lover.

7/6/72

In the early months of 1966, with Gilbert gone, Denise and I were naturally drawn to one another. For the entire year prior to this, the three of us had been virtually inseparable. Never before had I met two people with whom I had so much in common. Murray and I (and for a brief time, New York theater activist Victor Lewis) lived directly above Gilbert and Denise at our Burgundy Street apartment house in the French Quarter. Many an evening after working at the theater we would all share a meal at either of the two apartments, sometimes breaking out our musical instruments and joining together in song until late at night. From this vantage point, I had painfully witnessed the unraveling of my friends' marriage.

Out of loyalty to Gilbert, for whom I had enormous affection, I resisted the inevitable, but the feelings between Denise and me were too strong to deny. Just prior to starting that summer's tour, in spite of our best efforts not to, Denise and I became romantically involved. When the season ended, it was clear to both of us that the strain of the past year had drained our spirits of the energy and enthusiasm needed to continue our work with the Free Southern Theater and we decided, at long last, to leave FST and to move on with our lives. With John, Tom, and Big Daddy at its helm, FST would go on to continue its work and its struggle for survival for the next fifteen years, long after the civil rights movement which inspired it had ended.

Together, Denise and I headed for New York City, where we joined FST "friends" Swedish-born stage and screen actress Viveca Lindfors and writer-husband George Tabori for a touring production of an anthology of scenes and monologues compiled and edited by George entitled *Three Boards and a Passion*. The cast of four included Viveca, Denise, Harris Yulin, and myself. Under the direction of Gene Frankel (*The Blacks*), this rather slight and contrived concoction in which we each played a multitude of roles was far less fulfilling than FST had been and my work was flat and uninspired, but it was still a welcome change from what had become the burdensome task of running a theater with little or no money. The luxury of touring in a first-rate union production with all the amenities felt almost like a vacation after two years (three for Denise) of working and living on a shoestring.

After this tour of the Midwestern and Northeastern states, Denise and I returned to New York and investigated several workshops together, including those that were being run by teacher-director Joseph Chaikin, by Brooklyn-born actor-singer Lou Gossett, and also by an actor, director, and, to my mind, a most brilliant teacher hailing from Charleston, South Carolina, named Robert Macbeth. Denise and I went to see a small showcase production of two short plays at the old Elks Club on West 126th Street which had been mounted by Bob and his partner Allan Miller. The plays were unimpressive in and of themselves but featured a few of their prize students, most notably the young and amazingly gifted Helen Ellis, a native of Jamaica, West Indies (and the future Mrs. Macbeth), and Gary Bolling, a Harlem-bred actor who had first impressed me with his performance as Little Man in Shirley Clarke's 1962 film *The Cool World*. Seeing Gary's and Helen's work live and close-up in this small, intimate, bare-boned presentation was even more impressive. The power, intelligence, and spontaneity of their performances were startling, and I remember thinking "wherever this caliber of work is being done is where I want to be."

After attending a few sessions of Macbeth's workshop, Denise became disenchanted with his unconventional approach and decided to study with Joe Chaikin and his Open Theatre Company, eventually performing in their anti-war play, *Viet Rock* at the Martinique Theatre in early '67. Soon afterwards I was cast in a small role as a Hell's Angel biker in a short-lived play at the Cherry Lane Theatre entitled *Party on Greenwich Avenue* written by a fellow named Grandin Conover. It also featured a performance by Clarence Williams III playing a con man disguised as a nun. I spent that summer with a company called Theater-In-The-Streets which, under the direction of Group Theater and Actors Studio legend Phoebe Brand (wife to the renowned Shakespearean actor Morris Carnovsky), toured the boroughs of New York and Chicago presenting a repertoire of simple morality plays performed on an open truck in the city streets. The highlight of this engagement for me was the production of a play with masks entitled *Sholo* which was performed entirely in Spanish.

Unlike Denise, however, I had found Macbeth's workshops deeply compelling, with his blend of Actors Studio "method" and jazz-influenced avant-garde. Bob's approach to the dramatic arts was built around his strong appreciation for both the unique value of each individual artist *and* the ability to create a total fabric in which the subtle interaction among his players was paramount. With a masterful use of improvisation and music, he was able to elicit from his actors a powerful sense of spontaneity, collaboration, and creativity which liberated and propelled each of them to new heights of inventiveness and discovery.

But even more than his artistic prowess, Macbeth's vision of a new Harlem theater where this aesthetic sensibility could be used to "raise the consciousness" of our people struck me as being as cogent and inspiringly revolutionary an idea as the Free Southern Theater had a few years earlier. With experience in both the professional mainstream theater (*The Blacks*, *Tiger, Tiger, Burning Bright*, etc.) and also within the publicly and privately funded world of community-based cultural activism (the HARYOU ACT, Ford, and Rockefeller Foundations), Macbeth was poised to take full advantage of the prevailing tide of philanthropy at the end of the sixties.

At only twenty-three I had, as yet, no overwhelming desire to work within the mainstream entertainment industry, particularly with the new black cultural revolution in full swing. I was primed and ready for the challenge when, at the end of my stint with Theater-In-The-Streets, Bob asked me to perform in the maiden production of his newly founded New Lafayette Theatre. I was to play the lead role of Tim, Jr., in Detroit playwright Ron Milner's biting and insightful family drama, *Whose Got His Own*, cast opposite the wonderful Estelle Evans as Tim's mother Sarah (a character which she had originated the year before at the American Place Theatre). I had finally found in this play's young protagonist a role which addressed the complexities of my generation and which also thoroughly challenged me in my capacities as a dramatic

Scene from WHOSE GOT HIS OWN with Janice Fenner and Estelle Evans, 1967. (Courtesy of Robert Macbeth and New Lafayette Theatre Archives.)

actor. Returning home for the funeral and burial of his father, Tim, Jr., painfully but bravely confronts all the demons of his childhood including the scarred relationship between himself and Tim, Sr. Glynn Turman had played the role at American Place, and Barbara Ann Teer, who a few years later would found the National Black Theatre in Harlem, had played his sister Clara, a role now performed by Janice Fenner, a talented young student of Macbeth's.

By now, Bob and I had developed the beginnings of what would become the most intensely collaborative and influential relationship of my career, and working under his sure-handed direction, I was able to stretch my wings and fly in this role, capturing both critical and audience approval as never before. Upon reviewing the opening-night performance of Friday, October 13, 1967, at the theater's newly designed space on West 132nd Street (just adjacent to the original Lafayette Theatre of the 1920s and '30s where Hunter had performed), Earl Chisolm of New York's *Amsterdam News* said of my work, "Confused, powerful, seeking, destroying, and yet warm, even loving, Mr. Orman's interpretation is alone worth the trip." For the first time in my five years of acting I felt that I had attained the ability to handle virtually any role that might come my way. Within the New Lafayette, I had found a new home in which to do just that.

Meanwhile, downtown on Manhattan's Lower Eastside, Denise had established ties, both personal and professional, with Robert Hooks (who, with the recent release of Otto Preminger's *Hurry Sundown*, was emerging as the most visible black matinee idol in the country) and partners Gerald Krone and Douglas Turner Ward (whose recent double-bill offering of Ward's *Happy Ending* and *Day of Absence* was the longest running success in Black theater since *The Blacks*). The combination of Hooks' charming and charismatic star power, Ward's driving ambition, and Krone's business savvy had become a powerful new force on the theater scene.

Denise, along with other such talented performers as Moses Gunn, Frances Foster, Esther Rolle, Clarice Taylor, David Downing, Rosalind Cash, Norman Bush, William Jay, Allie Woods, Hattie Winston, and Judyann Jonsson, would help form the nucleus of the Negro Ensemble Company (NEC), a group with goals that were decidedly more "mainstream" than those of The New Lafayette and other black community-based theater companies of the era. And so, artistically and personally, our paths parted. With her pivotal association as a founding member of NEC and her eventual rise to Hollywood television and film stardom

New Lafayette Theatre Company members, L-R: Sonny Jim Gaines, Yvette Hawkins, Gary Bolling, Whitman Mayo, me, George Miles, Beverly Collins, Sam Wright, Helen Ellis, Bill Lathan, Peggy Kilpatrick, Roberta Raysor, Estelle Evans, Kris Keiser, Bob Macbeth, Bette Howard, Ed Bullins, Marvin X, 1968. (Courtesy of Robert Macbeth and New Lafayette Theatre Archives.)

(*Room 222, Blacula, Let's Do It Again, In the Heat of the Night*), Denise Nicholas would become among the more prominent African-American actresses of the next two decades. My own career would follow its own peculiarly unpredictable course.

Harlem of the late 1960s was a landscape upon which some of the most earth-shaking occurrences happened with amazing rapidity, not the least of which, of course, was the violent uprising of 1968 following the April 4th assassination of Martin Luther King, Jr., in Memphis, Tennessee. The murder of this messenger of love and world peace and its aftermath was surely one of the darkest moments in our history, when the rage and sorrow of an entire people engulfed our nation and poured into the streets. Appropriately, the ensuing saga of the New Lafayette Theatre had a potent mix of myth and legend attached to it and more than a little sense of drama.

The theater's second production, for which I served as stage manager, was a revival of *The Blood Knot*, renowned South African playwright Athol Fugard's two-character play about half-brothers (one black and the other of mixed race and fair-skinned), directed by Bob's friend and colleague Allan Miller, the New Lafayette's only major white collaborator. Allan, who had performed the play Off-Broadway opposite Douglas Turner Ward, had also briefly coached me in preparation for my work on *Whose Got His Own*, and we had developed a warm mutual respect for one another. Ably acted by Ed Smith and Nick Smith (not related), the play had a modestly successful four-week run.

Soon after this production, sometime during the early weeks of 1968, the theater's space was provided to the organizers of a symposium to discuss the provocative and scholarly tome by Harold Cruse, *The Crisis of the Negro Intellectual*. This gesture by Macbeth marked the beginning of a broader concept of the theater's role within the community, as a venue where vital matters such as art, politics, and economics could be vigorously debated. The *Crisis* panel included Larry Neal, Roy Innis, Bill Strickland, Charlie Russell, Preston Wilcox, and Sylvester Leaks, with a near-capacity audience made up mostly of artists, activists, and intellectuals of various stripes. The discussion became fairly heated and eventually led to a short scuffle among some audience members, resulting in the bodily eviction of a well-known community activist of questionable loyalties named Donald Washington. The evening was soon brought to a close, and after safely clearing the theater, Bob, company manager Ernie McClintock and I locked up and went home, which for me was less than two blocks away.

A few nights later, I was awakened by a loud knock at my door. It was assistant company manager Ron Walker with the news that someone had set fire to the theater. By the time we arrived, the interior structure of the building had been totally incinerated. Although no charges were ever brought against Washington, or anyone else, there was an unspoken but undeniable assumption of his involvement. So there we stood, in the wee hours of a cold January night, watching the flames devour what we had all hoped would be home to a new chapter in theater history. But, like the mythical Phoenix, the New Lafayette would rise again.

The third production at New Lafayette, after *Blood Knot*, was to have been *In the Wine Time* by Philadelphia-born playwright and West Coast political activist, Ed Bullins. Before the untimely destruction of our home facility, Bob had contacted Ed, who at the time was serving as Minister of Culture for the Black Panther Party in Oakland, California, and offered him the position of Playwright-in-Residence at the theater. Bullins was a strikingly talented and prolific chronicler of the contemporary African-American experience. *In the Wine Time* was just the first in a series of major works, interwoven and connected by character and theme, which Bullins had dubbed his "Twentieth-Century Cycle" of plays. It was, easily, one of the most ambitious ventures to be undertaken by a modern American playwright. In his wisdom, Macbeth knew that such a powerful and visionary body of work would well serve the aspirations of his theater.

But for now, during the first months of 1968, without a home base, at least temporarily, Macbeth and Bullins decided to venture downtown and, under the auspices of Wynn Handman's American Place Theatre, present three one-act plays of distinctly different styles and content, to mark the team's New York debut. *A Son Come Home* (a lyrical coming-of-age tale), *The Electronic Nigger* (an hilarious confrontation between two over-educated academics), and *Clara's Ole Man* (a caustic study

With Kelly-Marie Berry in CLARA'S OLE MAN, 1968. (Courtesy of Martha Holmes.)

in urban blight), provocatively presented under the collective title *The Electronic Nigger and Others*, opened at American Place in the spring of that year to rave notices from New York's critical establishment. This startlingly original and versatile display, in addition to introducing the Bullins/Macbeth team, also provided a glimpse of the nucleus of what would soon become the New Lafayette Players. For Gary Bolling, Helen Ellis, Estelle Evans, George Lee Miles, Kris Keiser, and me these plays served as an extension of the delicately tuned ensemble which we had begun to establish through several months of workshops as we awaited the site of our new Harlem home.

The role of Jack in *Clara* provided me with some subtly detailed character work unlike anything I had done before. An ex-Navy man naive in the ways of the streets who becomes increasingly inebriated during the course of the play, Jack tries (unsuccessfully) to navigate his way through the matrix of lies and half truths woven by his less than hospitable hostesses, the demure but beguiling Clara and the overbearing and dominating Big Girl. Helen was absolutely devastating as the tormented and inarticulate Baby Girl and there were also solid performances from Kelly-Marie Berry as Clara and Carolyn Cardwell as Big Girl. *The Electronic Nigger* was greatly aided by exceptional work in the two lead roles from Wayne Grice and L. Errol Jaye (a.k.a. Leonard Jackson).

After a successful limited run at the American Place Theatre's West

46th Street location in St. Clement's Unitarian Church, the plays were moved to the Martinique Theatre on 32nd Street (under the less incendiary title *The Ed Bullins Plays*) for an extended run. During this same period, through Bob's ongoing and increasingly intensive workshops, the remaining key company members were assembled: Sonny Jim Gaines, Whitman Mayo, Rosanna Carter, Yvette Hawkins, Roberta Raysor, Peggy Kilpatrick, Bette Howard, and a young physician/actor from Philadelphia named Bill Lathan.

It was also during this time of the Martinique run of Ed's plays, on a warm early April evening just before curtain time, that we all heard the news of the slaying of Martin Luther King, Jr. Struck literally numb with shock, the company convened and decided to proceed with the show in dedication to King. After the performance, no one could go home. Word soon arrived that actor Nick LaTour, son of legendary civil-rights leader E.D. Nixon, had invited us and others within the theatrical community to come to his apartment on 110th Street so that we could all commiserate and absorb the tragedy of the moment together. The gathering was an intensely somber affair in which no one knew quite what to say although some of those present expressed a foreboding sense of what might lie ahead. After a short while I headed for home. As I entered the subway at Lenox Avenue to travel the few short stops to my 132nd Street apartment, I could hear the beginnings of the rioting.

By the time that I ascended the subway stairs at 135th Street, the entire length of Lenox Avenue had erupted. Scores of mostly young people moved from storefront to storefront breaking windows, setting fires, seizing hoards of merchandise, and evading patrol cars that roamed the streets. As I walked past the Lenox Terrace Apartments, I ran into one of its residents with whom I had become friendly, the noted jazz historian and author Albert Murray. As an elder who had seen and experienced much in life including, I would imagine, episodes similar to this one, Murray expressed his dismay at this self-destructive venting of rage that would only bring more hardship to our community. Like the police who shouted in vain through bullhorns, Mr. Murray pleaded for everyone to go home. Eventually, I did walk home, where I watched the television coverage of this and all the other uprisings across the country. I sat there and wept for Brother Martin, one of the premier patriots of the 20th century, and for the soul of the nation for which he had died.

By that summer in '68 Bob had found a new site for the theater, the old Renaissance movie house on Seventh Avenue near 138th Street, located in a still vibrant area and adjacent to the long-renowned Renaissance Ballroom. Across the street from the popular Red Rooster night club and restaurant, it was also just around the corner from Adam Clayton Powell Jr.'s Abyssinian Baptist Church and within two blocks of the famously affluent Striver's Row. With continued support from McNeil Lowry of the Ford Foundation, Macbeth contracted a highly reputable architectural firm from downtown Manhattan to design and construct a beautifully versatile, contemporary theater facility in which to house The New Lafayette. Also around this time, two people were hired to handle the administrative and managerial responsibilities for the fledgling theatre company. Beverly Collins ran the office while Sam Wright oversaw the finances.

In the meantime, the acting company continued to fully prepare itself for the task ahead. We rented the space at One West 125th Street for more intensive workshops in acting and improvisation. We attended classes in martial arts with Sensei Moses Powell, vocal study sessions with Brooks Alexander, dance with Louis Johnson, and musical percussion with Nadi Qamar and Sonny Morgan. We even renewed ourselves with a week-long retreat to New England's Martha's Vineyard for a collective commune with nature. All of this preparatory work strengthened and sensitized us as a group, helping to mold us into a finely tuned acting ensemble.

Finally, on December 10th we christened our new home with the premiere of *In the Wine Time*, Ed's profane and beautiful rite of passage play, the first of his Twentieth-Century Cycle. Its three main characters, 16-year-old Ray, his uncle Cliff, and his aunt Lou, were vividly brought to life with extraordinary conviction by Gary, Sonny Jim, and Bette. The supporting roles were given equally commanding portrayals by Whitman, Peggy, Helen, Yvette, Kris, George, Roberta, Billy, and Estelle. I played the off-stage role of radio deejay Hep Harrison whose sensuous rhythmic patter and timely musical selections provided the soundtrack for this brutally poignant tale of sacrifice and redemption.

With this striking production it was clear to all that we were witnessing the emergence of one of the major playwrights of our generation. And the chemistry between Bullins' writing skills and Macbeth's directing prowess was truly breathtaking. These two men, both in their mid-thirties, were physical and temperamental opposites; Ed was short, muscular, dark-skinned, brooding, and silent; Bob was tall, light-skinned, athletically animated, and exceedingly articulate. Yet they shared a powerful compatibility based upon an obvious mutual respect and admiration for one another's talents, and the endlessly eloquent Macbeth, always the consummate director, made sure to develop and promote this relationship to its fullest effect. For his part, Bullins quietly set out to create one of the most impressive bodies of work in modern theater history.

For all of us, the entry into Bullins' world of familiar yet mysterious characters that were observed without sentimentality but with an honesty and a love supreme was like taking part in the creation of a new language that was both ancestral and prescient. Our hybrid form of ensemble acting, much akin to the esthetics of jazz music, lent itself perfectly to the freely interpretive style of these works. Consequently, I felt as if I had been born to play Steve Benson in *The Duplex*, Namor in *The Devil Catchers*, Soro in *The Psychic Pretenders*, and Art Garrison in *The Fabulous Miss Marie*, just a few roles that I originated at Lafayette. In fact, it eventually became apparent that Ed's characters were being specifically crafted to fit the unique qualities of each of his players.

For our part, the un-self-consciousness that emerged from this reciprocity resulted in a most extraordinary sense of freedom, enabling each actor to claim a legitimate ownership of his or her roles. Under Bob's masterful direction we became an ensemble of artists akin to the orchestras of Duke Ellington or Sun Ra, idiosyncratic, probing, able to play tight harmonies as well as virtuoso solos at will, yet always mindful of the larger context, the total fabric to which we were lending our voices. In short, we had become the perfect instrumentation to perform Ed's visionary compositions.

After *In the Wine Time* and a revival of *Whose Got His Own* with

George as Tim, Jr., and Helen as Clara, in April of '69 we presented the four-act revolutionary tragi-fantasy *We Righteous Bombers*. Written by Ed under the pseudonym of the fictitious (and deceased) Kingsley B. Bass, Jr., the play aroused considerable controversy with its irreverent depiction of a band of futuristic Harlem revolutionaries. In it, I played the central character of Murray Jackson, revolutionary poet and designated but reluctant assassin. Artistically and intellectually ambitious, though unwieldy, the production stimulated an unprecedented level of debate within the Harlem theatrical and activist communities. Again, as it had been in '68, the theater was offered as a forum in which to house this discussion. Chief among the play's detractors were Amiri Baraka, Larry Neal, and Askia Muhammad Toure, who each decried either the play's elements of counter-revolutionary sentiment, its adherence to archaic Western theatrical form, or both. Baraka and Neal had, just a few years earlier (1965), radicalized and electrified the Harlem theater community with the founding of their short-lived Black Arts Repertory Theatre/School, in the process igniting the fuse that would lead to the sudden explosion of urban black theaters here and around the country. They, along with Toure and others, were now entrenched in their philosophies of "revolutionary" protocol. In addition to the aforementioned transgressions, the play's main elements had apparently been "plagiarized" by Bass/Bullins from Albert Camus' *The Just Assassins,* a fact which, when discovered by our critics, offered more ammunition for their attacks.

In spite of its notoriety (and huge audience popularity) I personally found *Bombers* to be among the least satisfying of my acting experiences with The New Lafayette. With its desire to be intellectually sophisticated and politically "relevant," the piece lacked the usual level of fluidity and cohesion associated with Ed's writing as well as the subtle nuance of character and content which had become our company trademark. My own performance, although emotionally charged, was somewhat overwrought and lacking in conviction. It was definitely below my usual standards, a feeling which was underlined by one of the most scathing criticisms of my career in a review by Clayton Riley of the *Amsterdam News*. So affected was I by this first "bad" review that, although I cannot remember the specific basis of its criticism, these comments by Riley (who has since become a friend) are still taken by me as a painful reminder to adhere to the basic principles of my craft, a good lesson for any young journeyman or seasoned veteran.

In any case, we moved on. Bob, due in part to the discrediting of *Bombers*, decided that we would pursue the development of a new theatrical form with which we had been experimenting, called the ritual. In truth, it was not a totally new concept but one which reached back to our African ancestral roots and attempted to rekindle and strengthen the connection between the arts and the spiritual forces which rule our lives. It required, especially within our contemporary context, a radical redefinition of our collective and individual identities by summoning up a wealth of what Bob called our "historical race memory" and creating a newly consolidated spiritual consciousness.

This new journey also demanded from each of us an unprecedented level of trust and a commitment to collective discovery outside the conventions of theater as we all had come to know and practice them. To help achieve this goal, Bob enlisted the services of Dr. Ademola Olugebefola and some of his fellow visual artists who, in the early sixties, had founded and continued to manage the Weusi Art Gallery of Harlem on West 132nd Street (just a few doors down from the theater's original location). The esteemed Olugebefola, along with his exceptionally gifted colleagues Abdul Rahman, Bill Howell, Otto Neals, and others, began to transform our theater into a stunningly evocative environment, capable of housing this new and highly stylized form of expression.

Added to this extraordinary fusion was an assemblage of musical artists which included the likes of African drummer Chief Bey, reedman Pat Patrick, percussionist and flutist Sonny Morgan, African instrumentalist Nadi Qamar, bassist Naji Mulia Ibrahim, guitarist Louie Williams, drummer Al Harewood, and trumpeter Bruce "Khalil" Carmichael, among others. The talents and energies of all these splendid artists were painstakingly synthesized by Macbeth to create a hypnotic experience for our audience. From the moment that they entered our doors, the sounds, the smells, and the lighting designs all created an ambiance which transported them to a higher collective consciousness.

From late August to late September of 1969 we performed the first in the series, *The Ritual to Bind Together and Strengthen Black People So That They Can Survive the Struggle That Is to Come*. In monk-like fashion, all the men in the company shaved their heads for this production. (Later, this would become a permanent trademark for me, long before Michael Jordan and other "baldies" would set the trend in the eighties). Throughout the five-year existence of the theater, we continued to experiment, alternating between the ritual pieces: *To Raise the Dead and Foretell the Future* (March of 1970), *A Black Time for Black Folk* (August of the same year), and the more traditional dramatic form characterized by the Bullins Twentieth-Century Cycle plays: *Goin'a Buffalo* (October 1969), *The Duplex* (May 1970), and culminating in his masterwork and The New Lafayette's most widely celebrated offering, *The Fabulous Miss Marie*. With *Marie*, which opened on March 5th of 1971, the company had created a richly layered tapestry of behavior and characterization which represented a new level of the relaxed, spontaneous, and powerful virtuosity of expression for which we had become known. Its stylistic flexibility both within and outside the conventions of the imaginary "fourth wall" provided for a fascinating and provocative interplay among actors and audience.

We also performed two pieces by Ed which fell into a third category, combining elements of both the ritual and the conventional play forms. *The Devil Catchers* (November 1970) and *The Psychic Pretenders* (December 1971) were both highly stylized futuristic allegorical adventures, which stretched the concepts of time and place to much broader dimensions. Similar in feel to both the earlier samurai films of Akira Kurosawa and the later *Star Wars* movie sagas of George Lucas but with characters, themes, and cultural references specific to African-American experience, these mythic tales were, in my opinion, the most imaginative, ambitious, and high-spirited productions within our repertoire. Furthermore, they required our audience, through their use of metaphor and symbolism, to think beyond their simple precepts and to conceptualize on a much broader and, ultimately, more liberating scale. But, despite the creative fulfillment provided to us by these more adventurous works, it was also clear, however, that most of our audience preferred the naturalism of the more traditional stories and characters in the Cycle plays. In these productions they were able to see themselves and their world in vivid relief, projected in richly textured dimension, offering them a more accessible vehicle through which to contemplate and celebrate their collective existence.

During the latter few years of the theatre's existence, the space was also provided as a venue for musical concerts by some of the period's leading avant-garde artists, such as the Chicago-based Sun Ra and his Solar Arkestra (which featured our company's resident baritone player Pat Patrick). We also hosted performances by popular tenor saxophonist Pharoah Sanders, reedman Vishnu Reed, and vocalist extraordinaire Leon Thomas. The expansive stylistic forms of these artists complemented our own sense of freedom and exploration within the world of theatre.

The contrast between my experiences with The New Lafayette Theatre and the Free Southern Theater was profound in nature. Macbeth's deceptively simple company goal to raise audience consciousness or "to show our people who we are, where we are, and what condition we are in" proved to be extraordinarily ambitious and complex. Instead of building an arts institution to serve a specific political or social movement, as FST had done, the focus at New Lafayette was also revolutionary but in a truly cultural sense, with its collective art transcending the goals of traditional "protest" theater.

In this respect many of the Black Theater companies of this period shared a common objective: to explore new territory in the creation of an art that spoke directly to its audience. Within the confines of New York City alone there existed an abundance of talent and visionary leadership devoted to this end. Roger Furman's New Heritage Theatre of Harlem had been producing original works for a number of years prior to the founding of New Lafayette. Former New Lafayette production manager Ernie McClintock had gone on to found Harlem's Afro-American Studio for Acting and Speech, which not only mounted plays but also served as an educational institution dedicated to the training of aspiring young actors and technicians. Barbara Ann Teer's National Black Theatre, taking its cue from New Lafayette experimentations with the ritual form, expanded upon this concept and went on to secure substantial long-term funding for this work and for the construction of its new theater facility on Harlem's 125th Street. In the borough of Brooklyn the new movement was strongly represented by such institutions as The East, The Billie Holiday Theatre, The Bed-Stuy Street Academy, The Bed-Stuy Theatre, and The Brownsville Laboratory Theatre, among others. In addition to the unparalleled and far-reaching impact of Douglas Turner Ward's Negro Ensemble Company, audiences on Manhattan's Lower East Side also enjoyed the substantial contributions of Walter Jones's Cornbread Players, the multi-culturalism of Ellen Stewart's La Mama Experimental Theatre Club, and, of course, the now legendary magnanimity of Woodie King, Jr.'s New Federal Theatre.

As was true of most of these theaters, The New Lafayette's location and its decision to advertise only within the Black community (in spite of the theater's dependence upon white philanthropy for its existence) were clear philosophical choices within the black/white political scenario of the times. These theaters' single-minded creation and promotion of the Black Arts coupled with their resistance to almost all influences by white society other than its financial support, although temporarily advantageous, would prove, ultimately, to be an impractical and unsustainable policy of operation. Eventually, the well of benevolence would run dry. But for the time being, this arrangement afforded these companies, particularly The New Lafayette Theatre, a remarkable level of creative freedom. This exclusion of influence by whites was based upon and fueled by the need to rectify the centuries-old domination and oppression of the world's people of color in all facets of their existence. The Black Arts movement of the 1960s and '70s provided a diversity of American artists of African descent with the inspiration and the opportunity to find their own unique and distinctive voices based upon both their individuality and the wisdom of an ancient and powerfully resonant ancestry. And no other Black community-based theater of this era received a level of both financial patronage and autonomy to pursue its artistic vision equal to that of The New Lafayette.

With the exception of *We Righteous Bombers*, however, the primary focus of our work was within a Black cultural context, with little or no direct reference to white society. To some within Harlem's "Black

Power" movement this stance was interpreted as being either naive or dangerously misguided, but the issues and concerns within the "revolution" to which we were committed were, in our minds, larger, deeper, and more essential than those being raised by such polemicists, issues beyond the conventional or rhetorical symbols of political power. Engaged in a struggle to heal the minds and souls of our people, to us our critics' pejorative use of the term "art for art's sake" missed the point by underestimating the spiritually redemptive and consciousness-altering powers inherent in the arts. On this score alone, the work of Macbeth, Bullins, and The New Lafayette, in my opinion, remains among the least understood (and underestimated) of this entire period.

In addition, many (but not all) of the characters who inhabited Ed's plays (as well as a significant portion of our audience) were among the most disenfranchised and the least visibly represented segment of the Black Diaspora: pimps, prostitutes, street hustlers, wanderers, winos, and various members of the working poor. Our portrayal of these "unenlightened" masses was far from what many of our critics considered to be appropriate fare for a "Black revolutionary theater." Bullins' plays expertly revealed and explored the primal passions, struggles, and the "building of relationships" within this social milieu without the need for any intellectual commentary to justify their existence. Startlingly true to life, these characters and their stories spoke profoundly about the universal social and moral themes that are the traditional staple of the world's great art institutions. As a theater company, The New Lafayette aspired to that level of authenticity and artistry from within the context of the Harlem community of the late 1960s and early 1970s.

Personally, The New Lafayette and Ed's plays also provided me with several opportunities to further develop my talents at directing. First, after the run of the three plays at American Place, I directed a staged reading there of *Goin' a Buffalo*. I co-directed the premiere full production of this play with Bob the following year at The New Lafayette. Later, after we had acquired a separate space for rehearsals and workshops at 112th Street and Lenox Avenue, I staged a production there of *Clara's Ole Man* with our company members performing it for a short run. I directed two different productions of an early three-character play of

Ed's entitled *How Do You Do*, first with Gary, George, and Helen for a Black Panther benefit at the Fillmore East, and later for another event with three New Lafayette protégés: Andre Mtumi, Starletta DuPois, and Willard (Walik) Reese.

Toward the waning days of the New Lafayette, Ed and I founded The Black Troupe, a theater workshop in Queens, New York, with the help of my cousin and lifelong confidant Gary James; Bob's younger brother, production manager and lighting designer Toby Macbeth; close friend and acting protégé Tommy Hicks; and others. We conducted classes in both play writing and acting and over the course of a year produced an original theater piece, written and performed by our students under my direction.

Later, after The New Lafayette had finally closed its doors and I had just returned to New York from a stint of Hollywood film acting, I staged a musical revue by Ed, entitled *House Party*, at Wynn Handman's American Place Theatre. I was extremely fortunate to have a cast that included Mary Alice, Earl Hyman, Rosanna Carter, Gary Bolling, Verona Barnes, Andre Mtumi, Basil Wallace, George Miles, and Jimmy Pelham. The production was greatly enhanced by Pat Patrick's wonderfully eclectic musical score performed by a live band which included himself and other greats such pianist Cedar Walton and drummer Al Harewood. It also boasted an innovative set design by Kurt Lundell which included original murals by the legendary artist Romare Bearden. In spite of these great assets, *House Party*, by far the most ambitious and challenging venture of my career as a director, was less than totally successful as a theatrical experience and left me feeling disappointed, overwhelmed and, ultimately, disenchanted with the task of directing. During the last days of rehearsing this production, Bob Macbeth graciously agreed to assist me in the final stages of its mounting.

Actually, with each of my directing assignments, it had become more and more obvious to me that I received far more joy from acting than I did from directing and, consequently, was much better at it. In fact, I had and continue to essentially use all my directing experiences to further enhance my acting skills. Having always had a great respect for skillful directors, I have also had the good fortune of working with some of the best, including, in addition to Macbeth, Kahn, and Moses, Bill Duke, Lloyd Richards,

Michael Langham, Oz Scott, Bill Lathan, Hal Scott, Neema Barnette, Jon Stone, and Regge Life, among others. But I am forever indebted to The New Lafayette for five incredible years of repeatedly testing and expanding my acting skills in one wonderful play after another. It's the kind of opportunity that is virtually unheard of in American theater today. Whatever level of craft and expertise I now possess I owe to those invaluable years of continuously rigorous work and discovery.

From a personal financial standpoint, The New Lafayette had provided each of us with a relatively comfortable existence. Although minuscule by today's standards, the weekly salary of two hundred dollars that we received during most of the four years between 1968 and 1972 was about six times what I had earned with FST and a princely sum for a single person living in Harlem at the time. This salary afforded us the sense of security we needed in order to focus on our creative mission.

As an extension of and a complement to our main work of producing plays at The New Lafayette, Ed and I, along with Marvin X (with whom Ed had co-founded Black House, a theater in northern California) and Richard Wesley (Ed's yet-to-be-produced prize student), began *Black Theatre* magazine in 1968. It became a national forum for the dissemination of ideas and information pertaining to the Black Theater movement which had exploded throughout the country during this period. It contained regular contributions by some of the most influential writers within the Black Arts movement, including Larry Neal, Amiri Baraka, Sonia Sanchez, Ben Caldwell, and Askia Muhammad Toure. In addition to serving as the magazine's associate editor, I also reported regularly on the progress of The New Lafayette and, in so doing, helped to chronicle the history of the company during its five years of existence. I welcomed this opportunity to further develop my writing skills, which, up to that point, had revolved exclusively around the poetry and song lyrics which had become my own personal journal, of sorts. The following summation to my report for *Black Theatre* issue number 7 in the winter of 1971 was symbolic of the prevailing philosophical tone within New Lafayette and the Black Arts movement in general and an example of the extent to which we had separated ourselves from the prejudicial precepts of white American culture:

> *The general development of our work over the years has been characterized by our moving away from conventional western forms towards the construction of a freer, more direct Black framework of expression, allowing for the fullest realization of each individual artist, to effect an experience which is rich and varied in texture, attracting the senses to a collective awareness....It is this sense of the collective spirit which constitutes the strength of our art and makes it a vital and moving force within the cultural life of the Harlem community and within the universal Black consciousness.*

In addition to the magazine, Whitman Mayo and theater administrator Karen Allen Baxter had formed the New Lafayette Play Service, an agency designed to represent the growing number of new playwrights, both from within our own writing workshop (e.g., Wesley, J.E Gaines, OyamO, Martie Charles, and others) as well as those from other regions and theaters nationwide. To their great credit, Karen and Whitman sustained the agency's existence for several years beyond the life-span of The New Lafayette. Renamed Nasaba Artists' Management, Inc., it provided an invaluable service to many of us, actors and writers alike, during our transitions into the more mainstream theater, film, and television industries.

That transition could hardly have been more intense or poignant. The final months, weeks, and days of The New Lafayette Theatre's existence seemed both interminable and triumphant. Under Bob's wise and tempered guidance the company made no last-ditch efforts to revive itself or to hold on for dear life. Mournful though it may have been for us, this was, ultimately, a time of acceptance and gratitude. We had accomplished something unique and wonderful together, something which would live on in each of our memories forever. To have struggled and floundered, settling for anything beneath this standard, would have been demoralizing in ways that would have irreparably tarnished the image of such a shining legacy.

Indeed, within the full spectrum of my life's work, The New Lafayette Theatre stands at the pinnacle in terms of both the depth of its ambition and the uncompromised excellence of its execution. To this day, however, some thirty years later, the sublime nature of our achievement remains largely unheralded by theater historians, or anyone else, for that matter. Fortunately, there was some film documentation of our work. During the early stages of The New Lafayette's existence, a television production team from Germany produced a piece on us entitled *Harlem Theatre*, which highlighted our initial workshops and performance efforts. Much later in the theater's life, during the fall of 1971, with the help of our own film production team made up of cinematographer Karma Stanley, stage manager Jesse Boseman, soundman Sonny Morgan, and grip and cameraman Toby Macbeth, Bob created his own documentary. Entitled *Ritual Masters*, it was a montage of scenes which showed the entire company in the process of preparing for its production of *The Psychic Pretenders*.

Despite the existence of these two invaluable records, they are basically unavailable to the general public. In fact, the New Lafayette Theatre's lack of an archival repository of information and materials and, as explained previously, the mainstream media's generally inadequate and sporadic coverage of its work, has relegated it, along with countless other institutions from this period, to a status of non-existence within the current cultural memory. Add to this the painful and near-criminal neglect afforded the actual landmark of the theater and its surroundings, wherein the entire block between 137th and 138th Streets on Seventh Avenue has been in a virtually continual state of decline and decay since The New Lafayette's closing, and we have the recipe for a severe case of cultural amnesia even for many who were present and certainly for those who were not. It is, obviously then, up to those of us who actually experienced this fabled episode in theater history to document and pass on its story to the current generation, to inform and hopefully enhance the creation of their own unique legacies. My own recollections of the New Lafayette Theatre continue to fill me with both a supreme sense of accomplishment and an acute awareness of the unlimited possibilities of the creative human spirit.

In any overview of Black theater in the nineteen-sixties and seventies, one must acknowledge the pre-eminence of activist/writer Amiri Baraka (a.k.a. LeRoi Jones). Perhaps more than any other single individual, his influence permeated the entire spectrum of this movement and of the people who embodied it. Baraka's career has been a living, eloquent metaphor for a whole generation of Black artists. His influence began with the Off-Broadway successes in the early to mid-sixties (as LeRoi Jones) of particularly *The Dutchman, The Toilet,* and *The Slave* and then continued with his radical move to Harlem with Black Arts Repertory Theatre/School in 1965. It extended into the early seventies with the Chelsea Theatre's powerful Off-Broadway production of *Slave Ship* and his founding of The Spirit House Movers and Players in his native Newark, New Jersey. Certainly through his volumes of poetry, essays, literary and music criticism and his fire-brand articulation of the socio-political and cultural realities of his times he has remained a beacon of light to others for over four decades. Baraka's literary prescience, courage, and skill set a new standard for his contemporaries and immediate heirs: Adrienne Kennedy, Ed Bullins, Charles Fuller, Ron Milner, Richard Wesley, Paul Carter Harrison, OyamO, Ntozake Shange, Samm-Art Williams, Philip Hayes Dean, and August Wilson, to name a few.

Baraka's penetrating and provocative influence laid much of the groundwork for The New Lafayette Theatre, The Negro Ensemble Company, The New Federal Theatre, The New Heritage Theatre, The Afro-American Studio for Acting and Speech, The National Black Theater, and many others. Few if any of these institutions, however, shared in his passion for political activism. I first met Baraka in the earliest years of my career at the beginning of the 1960s when he was just exploding onto the scene. At that time, I had recently been deeply affected by his play *The Dutchman,* and I continue to be inspired by his ferociously poetic intellect and edified by his continued encouragement and appreciation of my own work.

For us at New Lafayette as well as countless others who participated in this movement of Black cultural awareness between the mid-1960s and the early 1970s, the climate of social upheaval and turmoil in America during these times had added a near-nuclear level of energy and vitality (and disarray) to our efforts. The volume and intensity of exploration within the world of Black art was at its highest since the Harlem Renaissance of the 1920s and 30s. Unlike in this earlier period, however, the Civil Rights successes of the sixties had created new opportunities which, ironically, would undermine our accomplishments or, at least, render them irrelevant to future generations. By the assimilation of our cultural identity into the mainstream of America, we would be lulled into a collective amnesia in regards to our remembrance and recognition of this important phase in our history. American popular culture has traditionally absorbed black forms of expression into its lexicon, but never so much as during and since the 1960s and '70s.

The Black Theater movement's lack of a cohesive vision which could have accommodated this assimilation and provided an economic philosophy to carry it into the future and retain control of its product would prove to be its undoing. Furthermore, the sense of rivalry and subsequent divisiveness that permeated our small world of Black Theater served only to make it smaller and weaker. There were lamentable occurrences in which members from one company would attend a performance by another and voice their disdain, sometimes even during the show. Regrettably, I must confess that New Lafayette company members were particularly culpable in this regard. In actuality, the unique strength of each of the premier companies, just in New York City alone, was formidable and sufficient to have sustained perhaps another decade of creativity, or more. These strengths were ultimately neutralized by the inability of the movement's leadership (Macbeth, Ward, Furman, Teer, King, etc.) to establish and promote an ongoing association which would have transcended the differences between them and created a common ground on which they could all stand and wage a serious battle for institutional survival.

It should also be noted that, as during the be-bop era of the 1940s and '50s, the period from the mid-1960s to the mid-1970s was a time when the permeation of drugs, particularly marijuana and cocaine, was all-pervasive within our culture. It is impossible to say exactly to what extent the content and quality of the art created throughout this period was affected by this fact, but certainly the use of narcotics had some cumulative impact upon the long-term institutional vision and stability of many companies.

Personally, I began experimenting with marijuana as early as 1963,

Bob Macbeth, Sonny Jim, and me in front of New Lafayette Theatre, 1970. (Photo by Bill Lathan.)

with my fellow students at Circle in the Square and elsewhere. This was as normal as sharing a cup of coffee at the time for many within the artistic communities. Rarely, however, did I combine this with work, although I knew of those who did so frequently. I learned fairly early in my career that trying to perform under the influence of drugs could have disastrous results. I smoked a marijuana joint one evening in Jackson, Mississippi, just before a performance of *Roots*. During the course of the play I came to believe with every fiber of my being that this was undoubtedly the best performance of my life. I marveled at how truthfully I was experiencing every moment of the play, and while in character as the elderly Ray, I relished the effect that I must have been having upon my mesmerized audience. Coming offstage, preparing myself to humbly accept the ardent congratulations of my fellow company members, imagine my surprise at the nearly unanimous response of "What the hell were you doing out there?" I never repeated this mistake, but, given what we know today based on modern scientific research, I can't help but wonder what the overall effect of drug use during the '60s and '70s has had upon my generation's ability to carry the legacy of our work to the next generation.

This being said, for those of us who were able to internalize and sustain the lessons of integrity, craft, and artistic inventiveness learned during this incredible period of exploration and growth and to thrive, there were enormous challenges to be met and gains to be made as we moved forward into the 1980s and '90s.

CHAPTER FOUR
Moving On

Spring Thing

Just before the edge of a fresh era
Straining through the last strands of sorrow's wintry wonders
In this wind filled spectacle of life
These tropical eyes glare laser-beams through the night
Illuminating city-life be-boppers, studs, grays, fays and gays,
 johns
and other impostors
Poppin' mamas in a cool dark curl on the other side of
 sunshine-
Faces filled with banana dreams
Creamed with schemes of glitter and gleam
Yet riding with the fear
Of failing time's test
For real-
Where the highest vision's vantage
Is below the mark of merit
For those masquerading minds
Who deal-
And who boil their own brew to the brim
Of concrete caverns-
Mercy me-
The edge is wedging nearer
The eyes are getting clearer
Determining the picture
A multi-minded mixture
Of feast and famine burning on the brow
And Spring a thing a' jammin' on the other side of now.

4/27/74

t the end of 1972 I decided to take a long overdue vacation and headed for the warm tropical breezes of St. Croix, Virgin Islands. Several cousins of mine, Jose and Lucille DaCosta and Lana Gibbons and her sons Anthony and Ricky, had recently migrated there and settled in Frederiksted. I was graciously afforded accommodations for an extended stay, during which I was able to recover from the demise of the New Lafayette, as well as from the deaths in '70 and '71 of grandparents Hunter and Nanny Wells. I had not, as yet, taken the time to fully absorb and reconcile these losses nor to reflect upon the depth and breadth of their meanings to me. In addition, I had also recently ended a romantic relationship of two years. Undoubtedly, I was in need of some relaxation and renewal.

Although Nanny had family roots in the Caribbean, this was only my second time visiting the Islands. In the summer of '69 Sonny Jim and I had spent a week vacationing in Nassau, Bahamas, where, within a few days of our arrival, we both contracted food poisoning after consuming healthy portions of the local favorite raw conch (smeared with hot peppers, no less) and spent the bulk of our remaining time there sick in bed. Needless to say, it was one of the less enjoyable trips I had ever experienced.

My solo excursion to St. Croix, on the other hand, could not have been more different. The transition from the frigid wintry winds of New York City to the breezy tropics could not have been more therapeutic. Spending the Christmas and New Year's season on this lovely and hospitable paradise complete with the traditional annual holiday carnival was the most healing remedy imaginable, restoring my body, mind, and spirit to superior condition.

Upon my return home, I was surprised to find out that old friend and colleague Gilbert Moses had made several attempts to contact me

Aunt Cora Lee Day visits me on the set of WILLIE DYNAMITE, 1973.

while I was away. He reportedly wanted me to play the lead character in a film project of his. In the intervening years since the days of FST I had seen Gilbert a number of times and had followed his remarkable career as a noted theater director of such plays as Amiri Baraka's *Slave Ship* and Melvin Van Peebles' Broadway success, *Ain't Supposed to Die a Natural Death*, among others. He, in turn, had often visited the New Lafayette and had witnessed much of my own evolution as an actor. Our mutual respect and admiration had, in the nearly seven years since we'd last worked together, seemingly not suffered from any remnant feelings of estrangement connected to our former relationships with Denise. I was extremely flattered and grateful to learn that he wanted me to star in his film directing debut.

The road to securing the title role in Universal Pictures' *Willie Dynamite*, however, was not as simple as Gilbert's wanting me. A meeting was arranged for me with David Brown, one of the two producers of the film, to discuss the role and for him to decide if I was even worth considering for such a challenging assignment. I had read the script by Ron Cutler based on a story by Joe Keyes about the rise and fall of a singularly ambitious New York pimp. In recent years a new black Hollywood prototype of such characters had emerged behind the advent of such films as *Superfly* and *The Mack*. In my opinion, however, the moral and political subtext of this script with its underlying themes of redemption and transformation added more depth to the genre which would later come be known as "blaxploitation."

The meeting with Brown went smoothly and a screen test in Los Angeles was scheduled within a few weeks. This test was also no "shoe-in" for me. I was up against some of the most highly respected actors of my generation from both coasts. Dick Anthony Williams, Glynn Turman, and a young Carl Franklin were also screen tested. Yet, according to Gilbert, the decision by him, Brown, and partner Richard D. Zanuck to hire me, was unanimous. I was delighted. Within weeks of my return from the sands of St. Croix, I was in the thick of Hollywood being groomed by Universal Studios for stardom while also assisting Gilbert in the selection of the film's large supporting cast.

The key role of Cora, Willie's primary antagonist and would-be love interest, had already been cast with the popular and highly respected actress Diana Sands. She had first come to national attention some fourteen years earlier as Beneatha, younger sister of Sidney Poitier's character Walter Lee, in both the Broadway and film productions of Lorraine Hansberry's *A Raisin in the Sun*. I had also seen her star performance in the 1965 Broadway premiere of *The Owl and the Pussycat* opposite Alan Alda. When Gilbert told me she would be my co-star in the film, I felt honored to have the opportunity to work with this legend and my interest in the project became greatly enhanced. Before filming began, Gilbert, Diana, and I met at her Westside Manhattan apartment for a few bonding sessions in which we discussed the film, our characters, and life and art in general. I soon became totally transfixed with anticipation about going to Hollywood.

My only prior visit to Hollywood had been in 1966 during a brief assignment between my two FST seasons. John had asked that I represent the theater at a few fund-raising events hosted by several West Coast theater friends, including nightclub owner Ed Pearl, his choreographer wife Kate Hughes, and movie and television actor Tony Franciosa. At that time, the abrupt transition from the spirited and earthy idealism of the civil rights movement and its people to the superficiality, condescension, and cynicism of Tinseltown's industry folk was more than a little unsettling and intimidating.

This first trip would have been even more of a blow to my spirit of idealism had it not been for the grounding influence and the loving support I received from the Pearls, and also from my recently migrated aunt, actress-singer Cora Lee Day, and from two renowned members of the Los Angeles theater community, the maternally wise Frances Williams and the imposingly eloquent Maya Angelou. I was especially grateful to Maya for coming to my defense when attacked condescendingly by one of Franciosa's wealthy guests who labeled me as part of a "ragged band of young, unaccomplished amateurs." Seeing that I was at a loss for words, the majestic Ms. Angelou, with a calm and measured tone of voice, proceeded to tongue lash this supercilious bigot with a smooth and devastating precision that could aptly be described as "righteously elegant." She thus became, and remains, one of my great heroines.

This time, however, my experience couldn't have been more different. Less innocent, more worldly-wise, and a gainfully and very visibly employed lead actor in a major studio production, suddenly I was "somebody." I was deserving (at least for the time being) of the attention and respect of all those status-conscious industry insiders who had earlier dismissed me as naive and insignificant. Well, almost all.

Casting director Reuben Cannon, who had been responsible for hiring the majority of the film's supporting players, granted me a brief meeting to, ostensibly, discuss possible future projects. Instead, Reuben, who in 1973 was unquestionably the fastest rising black casting director within the Hollywood studio system, took the opportunity to make it clear that he would in no way provide even a hint of favoritism to me or to any of the worthy colleagues whose names I had naively mentioned to him in hopes of offering them a helping hand. "I started with nothing," he chided, "and pulled myself up by own bootstraps. Nobody ever helped me." It was my first encounter with Hollywood's version of the "I've got mine, you get yours" mentality which so permeates the entertainment industry, especially among blacks.

On a much more encouraging note, the film's head publicist, Collette Wood, had devoted herself, personally, to the promotion of my movie debut, with special attention paid to the national black media. Veteran hair stylist Robert Louis Stevenson perfected the shaved head and goatee look I had adopted to complement Bernard Johnson's extravagantly luxurious costumes for Willie's flamboyant persona. Ultimately, the net effect of this "rising star" treatment was to heighten my appreciation of the collaborative process which Gilbert had set into motion among the cast and crew. I felt privileged to be at the center of what was, for me, an exciting new Hollywood universe.

I had always loved the movies; from the earliest days of television and its airings of the classic bio-dramas starring Paul Muni (my all-time favorite movie actor), Henry Fonda, Jimmy Stewart, and Gary Cooper, the gangster sagas of James Cagney, Humphrey Bogart, and Edward G. Robinson and the thrilling Western horse operas with heroes such as Hoot Gibson, Ken Maynard, Johnny Mack Brown, Bob Steele, Tim McCoy, Lash LaRue, and my favorites, Hopalong Cassidy and Roy Rogers. As a little boy in the early 1950s, I even got to meet Roy, along with Dale Evans, Gabby Hayes and Trigger, when Nanny took me to a Gimbel's department store promotion.

Many a Saturday afternoon was spent at the Freeman Theatre, on Southern Boulevard in the Bronx, where I would sit spellbound by the five-feature presentation offered for a mere twenty-five cents. Like many boys of our generation, my friends and I had spent countless hours pretending to be the celluloid heroes of our favorite Western, gangster, or war movies. And now, here I was at the age of twenty-nine acting out a childhood fantasy by starring in the title role of an actual Hollywood "gangster" film.

On a more objective and professional level, though, I became an instant student of film acting. I learned, during the three-month shoot, volumes about the differences between film acting and acting before a live theater audience. I might have learned faster had I opted to attend some of the daily screening sessions of the previous day's footage, but, fearful of becoming too self-conscious, I avoided viewing my work until the end of filming. Intuitively, however, I learned that the most significant difference from stage acting, besides the absence of a live audience, was in the camera's microscopic attention to, and amplification of, the most subtle and minute actions and reactions. The basic techniques involved in the creation of a character's inner life and "motivation" are essentially the same in either medium. But in film, unlike on stage, all movement is greatly magnified, and even the slightest bit of mugging or exaggeration of expression can be read as false or overstated. Unfortunately, it took me weeks to absorb this lesson and to begin to develop the skills of underplaying inherent in good film acting. But once these were learned, my work became infinitely more effective and enjoyable.

Fittingly, one of my last days of shooting was for the final scene between Willie and Diana's character Cora after everything has fallen apart for both of them. For the first time in the film they are left to face themselves and each other without pretense or disguise. It's the scene where I feel I came the closest to attaining the kind of openness, sensitivity, and stillness that I've observed in the best of film acting and toward which I had been striving for months.

As a finished product, *Willie Dynamite*, could hardly be considered a great work of art. But neither was it as crass or unskillful as the average "blaxploitation" movie of its era. A solid storyline, combined with the abundant energy and talent of its novice director and a musical score composed by jazz great J.J. Johnson with original songs which were written by Gilbert and performed by Martha Reeves, elevated the film to a cut above average. It also boasted an unusually well seasoned cast: a mixture of both East and West Coast veterans of theater and film, which included Roger Robinson, Thalmus Rasulala, Norma Donaldson, Albert Hall, George Murdock, Marilyn Coleman, Clarice Taylor, Royce Wallace, and Robert Earl Jones, as well as the talented and exquisite young actresses Joyce Walker and Denise Gordy.

Tragically, however, this film would be Diana Sands' last. Halfway through filming, and unbeknownst to all but a few of us, she was diagnosed with cancer. She was advised to take a short break from work, and filming stopped for several weeks until she felt well enough to continue. She then completed work in her typically brilliant fashion, only to die shortly before the film's release early in '74. Both before and during the filming of *Willie Dynamite*, in my getting to know Diana I came to love and respect her as a friend, and her death hit me hard. In retrospect, the quality of Diana's performance after her hiatus had taken on a heightened intensity and emotional vulnerability, raising the quality of all of our work. So shocked and unsettled was I by her death that, regrettably, I couldn't even bring myself to attend her memorial service. I was absolutely grief stricken. I am immeasurably grateful to Gilbert for giving me, among other things, the opportunity to have known and worked with one of the great ladies of stage and screen.

Willie Dynamite would go on to receive relatively favorable reviews in the national press and media. It was marketed and distributed in much the same way as its recent predecessors only with less fanfare since the current wave of black urban dramas was already on the decline. The negative criticism of these films by many within the black "establishment" had given Hollywood an excuse to pull back from this "affirmative action" experiment. These low-budget productions had, in fact, already served their purpose by rescuing the nearly bankrupt movie industry of the 1960s, a mission that would be completed by the new wave of visionary white directors (Spielberg, Lucas, Coppola, Scorsese, etc.) who had begun to revolutionize and remodel both the aesthetics and the economics of the old studio system.

Willie Dynamite had been filmed for around one million dollars, which in 1973 was above average for its genre. Most of that money had, obviously, been spent on production costs, since as its star I was paid a whopping $12,000. This film could easily make a reasonable profit without promoting it beyond the usual black circuit of movie theater chains. The Richard D. Zanuck/David Brown team had also just produced the Paul Newman/Robert Redford blockbuster *The Sting*, which occupied the majority of their promotional attention (and dollars). The soon-to-emerge cable television and video markets would add even more profits to the coffers of these and other Hollywood production companies. The banner of Zanuck and Brown, interestingly enough, has been responsible for some of the better and more commercially successful films of the last thirty years, including *Jaws, Patton, M*A*S*H, Cocoon, Driving Miss Daisy,* and *Deep Impact*, to name a few.

As for the black experience on film, it would be another decade before filmmakers such as Spike Lee, John Singleton, the Hudlin and the Hughes brothers, Carl Franklin, Charles Burnett, Bill Duke, and others would develop the craft, the industry savvy, and the creativity to bring black cinema to the next crucial level. Like earlier black filmmakers such as Oscar Micheaux and Spencer Williams in the 1930s and '40s, this new wave of directors in the '80s and '90s would open more doors for the next generation of talent to emerge. In the meantime, a host of actors such as Ron O'Neal, Max Julien, Rosalind Cash, Robert Hooks, Vonetta McGhee, Calvin Lockhart, Gloria Hendry, William Marshall, Bernie Casey, Sheila Frazier, Thalmus Rasulala, and others who had begun promising film careers during this period in the early '70s would be denied any real opportunity to capitalize upon these experiences and to build the kinds of careers afforded many white actors with similar credentials. With the exception of Sidney Poitier, who was already in the middle of a two-decade reign as the one and only African-American movie star, Hollywood would turn a cold shoulder to any others who might aspire to such heights.

As for myself, although somewhat disappointed by Hollywood's lack of follow-up opportunity after a respectably auspicious film debut, I was thankful and happy to have had the experience and to return to New York where I would receive a load of offers from a still burgeoning and viable black theater world in which to challenge myself and expand upon the formidable skills that I had acquired. In truth, the best was yet to come.

CHAPTER FIVE
Sowing (Sesame) Seeds

AUTUMN

At these crossroads
Where inverted dreams
Promise to fruit fresh views
Yesterday's news falls
Like amber leaves
Into the beam of a new moon
And in the wee hours
We adjust to the justice
On our souls
Handed down by the grand and
The great grand 'cestors
Their unsung deeds
Haunting our autumn nights
With a deep and dark vision
To charge our hearts
With rhythm's precision
Perceived in the passion of summer moons
Sung to the tunes
Found in the sounds
Behind our brains
Within our words
Inside our eyes
Where the unborn dwell
In destiny.

And the hawk
Is steady
Breakin' down.

9/6/74

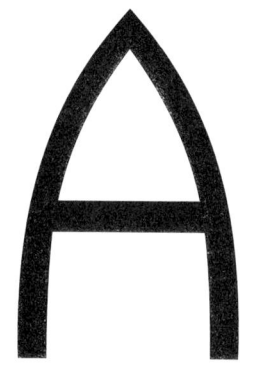mong the more exciting aspects connected with my new-found notoriety as the star of a Hollywood film was the confidence, self-esteem, and sense of luck that went hand-in-hand with such attention. But my incredible good fortune in meeting and wooing the beautiful and charming flower of the deep South who would become my wife and the mother of our four amazing children was obviously the work of divine intervention. Sharon Delores Joiner of Mobile, Alabama, strolled past the New Lafayette Theatre and into my heart one early spring day in 1973 like an apparition and changed my life forever. It was truly love at first sight, although it wasn't until my return from a trip to California later that summer that my heart was fully certain of our pre-destiny. Becoming a husband and father and going on to share with her in the creation of our family has become the single most defining element of my adult life, outlining and establishing the foundation for all of the joys and the sorrows of the years that have followed. It's hard to imagine what my life might otherwise have been.

New York City, whether it be Greenwich Village, the Lower East Side, Broadway, or Harlem, was, and still is, the cultural mecca of the world. Never was this fact more clear and comforting than when returning home to the "Big Apple" from the cultural wilderness of Hollywood fiefdom. My foray into movie acting, pleasurable as it was, had also heightened my appreciation for the art of live theater and its immeasurable rewards to actors of imagination and creativity. Although challenging and exciting, I had found the experience of working on *Willie Dynamite* to be somewhat tedious and artistically frustrating. By comparison, my return to the New York theater community was immensely liberating. Unexpectedly, however, my Hollywood baptism would serve as a source of both envy and admiration from many within that world, leading to a string of some of the choicest and most challenging roles of my career.

Sharon and me in Greenwich Village, 1974.

First came the offer from The Negro Ensemble Company's manager Steve Carter to replace Robert Hooks, who had in turn replaced Al Freeman, Jr., in the 1974 original production of Paul Carter Harrison's *The Great MacDaddy*. My role in this high-spirited allegorical fable was that of Scag, a flamboyant, multi-faceted, chameleon-like villain opposite Cleavon Little's stoically heroic title character. In addition to the extremely demanding physical nature of the role, I also had great fun with the flashes of satirical wit that were generously laced throughout Harrison's play. Cleavon, a Texas native and Tony Award winner for his starring performance in Broadway's *Purlie*, had recently scored in Hollywood even bigger than I with his lead role in Mel Brooks' enormously successful comedy *Blazing Saddles*. A fellow Gemini, Cleavon was a delight to work with, and together we were like opposite sides of the same coin, enjoying a chemistry reminiscent of that which I had shared with George Lee Miles through many of our New Lafayette incarnations. Within *MacDaddy*'s large company, I also had the great pleasure of working for the first time with such talents as Charles Weldon, Sati Jamal, Marjorie Barnes, Phylicia Ayers-Allen, Graham Brown, Judy Dearing, Saundra Sharpe, and Bebe Drake Hooks, to name a few.

Immediately after *MacDaddy*, my good friend and fellow Lafayette alumnus Dr. Billy Lathan asked that I play the pivotal role of Duane

Carter, jazz side-man and estranged husband to Veronica Redd's lead character Mavis Carter, in his production of Richard Wesley's *The Sirens* at Lynne Meadow's Manhattan Theatre Club. This was to be only the first of three plays by Wesley that I would premiere at MTC over the next fifteen years.

I had long admired the talent and intellect of my New Lafayette friend and colleague from Newark, New Jersey. One of Richard's early one-act plays was a two-character piece entitled *The Past Is the Past,* which explored the reunion of a father and the son he never knew. A day or two after its completion he handed it to me in the lobby of New Lafayette to take home and read. That evening I sat in my Harlem apartment and cried in recognition of our stories, both his and mine, as young black men who had not known their fathers. Richard was both an astute essayer of humanity through his plays and also an articulate spokesman for the concerns of black theater artists. Particularly impressive was his ability to render some of the most compelling and sensitive portrayals of contemporary male-female relationships to grace the stage, in such works as *Goin' Thru Changes, Gettin' it Together*, and *Black Terror.* To have finally been assigned a role as one of Richard's emotionally and intellectually complex young anti-heroes, especially in a play that was essentially about the liberation of women, represented an arrival for me at a new level of the "sensitive leading man" category which had, to some extent, been my stock-in-trade during the New Lafayette years.

Working under Billy's direction after having directed him several times during those earlier years was both amazingly effortless and fruitful, laying the groundwork for what would be a major collaboration for us some two decades later. In addition to a riveting lead performance by Veronica, there was stellar work from Loretta Greene (later replaced by Phylicia Ayers-Allen) and from the young and gifted Debbi Morgan. While performing in *Sirens*, I was also understudying both Dick Anthony Williams and Gylan Kain in Woodie King's production of Ron Milner's *What The Wine Sellers Buy* for Joseph Papp's Mobile Theatre Unit. Fortunately, only once did I actually have to go on for Gylan, calling upon my understudy, old friend George Miles, to cover for me as Duane.

One evening backstage, after a performance of *Sirens*, Billy Lathan's younger brother Stan, an accomplished and fast-rising director of film and television who would later go on to enormous success in Hollywood as the producer and director of the *Roc* TV series, *Def Comedy Jam*, *Def Poetry Jam*, and more, suggested that I try out for a recently vacated role on a children's TV show for which he had frequently worked. I had never actually seen the five-year old *Sesame Street*, but was aware of it, mainly through Billy's and Stan's Philadelphia childhood buddy, Matt "Buzzy" Robinson, who had served as both a writer and producer on the show. I knew Matt also to be the writer and/or producer of the films *Amazing Grace* and *Save the Children*. Surprisingly, he had also originated and performed the central role of Gordon on *Sesame Street* for three years, which, after two years of then being played by an actor named Hal Miller, was once again being recast by the show's producers, the Children's Television Workshop, hopefully for the last time. My first reaction to Stan's proposal was one of dismissal. After all, I was a serious dramatic actor, not a children's performer, which conjured images in my mind of Pinky Lee or Captain Kangaroo. Nevertheless, given the fact that Sharon and I were at the time expecting our first child, I reluctantly agreed to look into this possibly "steady paying gig."

To my surprise, the initial mutual response to the first meeting between *Sesame Street* producers David Connell and Jon Stone and me was one of intellectual engagement and genuine respect, something I had experienced only rarely within the television industry. Stone, one of the show's original creators, impressed me as a multi-faceted visionary much in the same vein as Bob Macbeth and Gilbert Moses had been, only with television instead of theater as his medium. I was asked by him and Connell to return for a screen test the following week. By then the field had been narrowed down to three finalists for the role, each a strong and well-seasoned contender. David Downing, one of NEC's original founding members, who had created, among many others, the title role in *The Great MacDaddy* which Cleavon had inherited, was an actor of genuine charm and intellect who possessed a sweetness of character, and a generous, unassuming quality which would seem to have been the perfect match for the good-natured Gordon. The other finalist was Robert Guillaume, a performer of considerable gifts, who would go on to fame and acclaim in stage, film, and television, most notably as the title character in the TV series *Benson*. Although I knew, liked, and admired both David and Robert, I thought Robert's persona a bit too urbane and aloof for the role, as opposed to David's easygoing and engaging charm. I considered my own chances to be about fifty/fifty.

Our screen test, however, was comprised of two parts. The first required us to do a mostly scripted scene with one of the Jim Henson Muppet characters on the show, Oscar the Grouch. This was truly a challenge for me, and probably for each of the others as well. Relating to, and performing with a puppet requires a suspension of disbelief quite unlike anything that most actors will experience throughout their careers. Caroll Spinney, who operates and performs Oscar (as well as Big Bird), was in complete and obvious view inside of Oscar's trashcan as I played the scene with him. As Oscar harassed me with such pleasantries as "Get away from my can," "You're botherin' me," or "Scram, and have a rotten day," I tried (not very successfully, I thought) to pretend that Caroll was not there and that this grungy green shag rug with eyeballs on the end of the puppeteer's arm was an actual person with whom I was to interact. Frustrated to say the least, I felt less than confident about my performance.

The second part of the test, however, involved working with a child in a semi-improvisational skit in which we had to convey a simple concept (up and down) in a humorous but educationally effective manner. Well, the child selected, for my test at least, was little John-John Williams, the brightest, most adorable five-year-old I'd ever met, who (unbeknownst to me) had already endeared himself to millions of parents and their children with his now classic one-on-one exchanges with such Muppet characters as Grover, Cookie Monster, and Kermit the Frog. I relaxed and had great fun with John-John and, needless to say, felt much better about this part of my audition. But, due to my feelings of inadequacy about the scene with Oscar, I went home with little hope of being offered the part.

Given this mind-set of resignation and acceptance of defeat, the call from executive producer Dulcie Singer a few days later, informing me of my selection for the role, was all the more stunning. A steady TV job with an annual salary of $20,000 was certainly a blessed gift for Sharon's and my newly expanding family. It was the late spring of 1974, and having just turned thirty, I was obviously experiencing another passage in life and moving into new and uncharted waters, both personally and professionally.

...on and... ...ance of defeat, the... ...executive producer Dulcie Sing... days later, informing me of my selection fo... ...was all the more stunning. A steady TV job w... ...nnual salary of $20,000 was certainly a bles... ...for Sharon's and my newly expanding family. ...the late spring of 1974, and having just tur... ...ty, I was obviously experiencing another pass... ...life and moving into new and uncharted wate... personally and professionally.

CHAPTER SIX
Reaping the Harvest

...with all blessings in life, my good fortune ...ring a regular role on an already established ...ected television show and also being introdu... ...he joys of fatherhood brought with it the equa... ...rtant responsibilities and challenges inherent ...of these positions. In both cases I had bec... ...nstant role model, within my own family as well ...he world at large. This held especially true w... ...oduction like Sesame Street in which all of ...an hosts" have come to represent surrogate par... ...res of sorts for millions of children across ...ed States and abroad. Along with the other c... ...ers, Will Lee, Bob McGrath, Loretta Long, So... ...ano, Emilio Delgado, Northern Calloway, Li... ..., Alaina Reed (and later Alison Bartlett, Sav... ...er, Bill McCutcheon, and David Langston Smyr... ...uld become a familiar face in the homes of ch... ...and parents everywhere. To our audiences we w... ...but were viewed as trusted friends and ...models, educators and chi... This rede...

FIRST FRUIT OF WINTER

Long awaited earth
We longed for the birth
of your eyes to smile to
and dream about without
waiting in doubt or wonder
We knew that you'd
defy our reason
and open the season
of future hope to
our hearts
And like the fruits of
a sacred soil you
sprang straight into the
streaming rainbow rush
Rasheda Gayle
Radiant Girl
of winter.

12/21/74

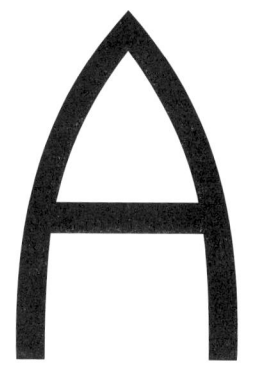As with all blessings in life, my good fortune in securing a regular role on an already established and respected television show and also being introduced to the joys of fatherhood brought with it the equally important responsibilities and challenges inherent in each of these positions. In both cases I had become an instant role model, within my own family as well as in the world at large. This held especially true with a production like *Sesame Street* in which all of us "human hosts" have come to represent surrogate parent figures of sorts for millions of children across the United States and abroad. Along with the other cast members, Will Lee, Bob McGrath, Loretta Long, Sonia Manzano, Emilio Delgado, Northern Calloway, Linda Bove, Alaina Reed (and later Alison Bartlett, Savion Glover, Bill McCutcheon, and David Langston Smyrl), I would become a familiar face in the homes of children and parents everywhere. To our audiences we were not actors but were viewed as trusted friends and endearing role models, educators and childcare advocates. This redefinition of my job definition and community status had a humbling, inspiring, and challenging influence upon me.

Joan Ganz Cooney, through her production company, The Children's Television Workshop (the creators of *Sesame Street* and its "graduate" program, *Electric Company*), was in the process of revolutionizing children's television. These shows' visionary use of the medium was helping to stimulate and inform millions of young minds, not just for the rudiments of early cognitive skill development, but also for learning how

Rasheda at age 1, 1976.

to live in the new multi-cultural world envisioned by the sixties generation. Both shows presented a diverse tapestry of ethnicity in which each cast member had equal stature regardless of heritage or gender. This was a radically new concept for American television and one which, unfortunately, has been only rarely duplicated since.

But in addition to becoming a recognizable and revered icon of family and community values, I had also become an actor whose loss of anonymity threatened to take its toll upon my craft. Like many within my profession, I had always found stimulation and fulfillment in the creation of a variety of characters who were distinctly different from me. These "masks," in effect, serve as shields and filters through which we actors explore and share some of the most revealing aspects of human existence, which, when blended with our own life experience, allows for the most subtly textured and compelling form of storytelling. An actor's ability to observe both himself and others un-self-consciously, to "disappear" and move through the world, absorbing the life around him, unimpeded by fame or notoriety, is an invaluable asset. I not only had new visibility as a TV personality, but this specific kind of visibility was about to change, as I would soon discover, the parameters of my life's work, especially in television. My entire career would now be affected by the issue of preserving the integrity of a production and a character which had come to represent a symbol of trust among its viewers, young and old alike.

In addition to the sense of security and fulfillment derived from being a part of a program such as *Sesame Street*, one of the more appealing aspects of the job was, and still is, the production schedule. Unlike most of series television, the entire season of shows is taped within a condensed and highly productive period, usually between four to five months. The remaining seven or eight months of each year are then available to the cast and crew to pursue other opportunities, as long as the other jobs do not conflict with the show's taping schedule. I immediately and enthusiastically took advantage of this considerable time, and within my first few seasons on *Sesame Street* found a range of employment in television and theater which marked a new level of activity within my career. As for TV, in addition to guest-starring on such shows as *Kojak* and *Sanford and Son* (what an absolute blast I had working with the hilarious Redd Foxx!), I was offered a role on the ABC soap opera *All My Children*.

All of these TV jobs, including *Sesame Street,* required that I be a member of both The American Federation of Television and Radio Artists (AFTRA) and Screen Actors Guild (SAG), the sister unions to Actors' Equity Association. I had, as the rules dictated, been allowed to work on *Willie Dynamite*, my first film, without becoming a member of SAG, but *Kojak*, also produced under their jurisdiction, required that I join them as well. So now in 1975, I had finally attained full membership in all of the actors' labor unions.

I was originally slated for only a few brief appearances on *All My Children*, just enough to help establish some background reality for a new regular character on the program (Donna Beck, played by Candice Earley). My character, Tyrone, was a viciously sadistic pimp whose main object of brutality was the young and misguidedly smitten Donna. Tyrone made Willie Dynamite look like a boy scout by comparison, and, after a year of playing the wholesome and reliable Gordon, I attacked the role with relish, eager to prove to a national TV audience that Roscoe Orman was an actor of range and versatility.

To the surprise of everyone, including myself, *AMC*'s fans responded overwhelmingly to the new and controversial story line (the first in daytime drama to feature such an explosive relationship between a black and a white character). The reaction to my performance was so sensational that the show's creator and head-writer, the legendary Agnes Nixon, asked that I sign an extended contract for one year, during which Tyrone would be quickly elevated to the status of major TV villain. With little hesitation, I welcomed this uniquely challenging opportunity to simultaneously display, on daytime television, two sharply contrasting character portraits, each at an opposite end of the spectrum; one intelligent, warmhearted, and likable, the other chillingly manipulative, seductive, and deadly. This was an actor's dream, I thought. It might even garner me a level of respect reserved for those few within my profession who had earned the title of "leading character actor," a designation labeling them as capable of playing virtually any role with power and conviction. I was, in fact, featured in a few soap opera magazines which highlighted this unprecedented dual feat.

I was to discover, however, that such recognition was both fleeting and shallow. Toward the end of this "dream" season I was, to my surprise and dismay, told by the producers of *Sesame Street* that I could no longer continue this display of versatility and must choose between my two jobs. It was explained to me that among the viewers of *All My Children* were parents and caregivers of kids who watched *Sesame Street*. These mostly female viewers (although I would come to discover that a surprisingly high percentage of soap opera fans are males) could, at the switch of a dial, see the same actor who'd just been playing with Big Bird and "babysitting" their kids suddenly and horrifyingly brutalizing defenseless young women. The sight of "Gordon" behaving so abhorrently out of character sent shock waves through households across America. Letters and phone calls had poured in, I was told, denouncing CTW and myself for inflicting such pain and disillusion upon the minds of the young and impressionable viewers of the show who (apparently like many adults) were unable to distinguish between real life and the pretended behavior on television.

After getting over the initial shock, my feelings were decidedly mixed. On the one hand, I resented being told that as a professional actor I suddenly had to place limits upon my creative freedom and play only roles that were deemed fitting to my new wholesome image. I had spent years resisting being told what I could or could not do in order to develop my skills as fully as possible. On the other hand, I could understand how some of the viewing public might not understand that I am an actor who can play many different kinds of roles, some mean, some nice, some comic, or whatever. More importantly, I could also understand as a parent the damage inherent in my presenting, however unintentionally, such harshly conflicting images to the young and fertile minds of *Sesame Street*'s targeted pre-school audience. Consequently, both for reasons of job stability, as well as those of moral responsibility, the problem of which role to choose became a "no-brainer." Although challenging and engaging, Tyrone was, essentially, an unredeemable "bad guy" who would eventually be eliminated, either by incarceration or death (he was, in fact, arrested after assaulting and attempting to murder the romantic lead, Dr. Chuck Tyler).

Gordon, by contrast, was, in addition to being an already established mainstay on a hugely successful show, the personification of many of the qualities which had been so severely lacking in the traditional representation of African-American males in film and television. As a loving husband (and eventual father), sportsman, amateur musician, science teacher, and loyal friend to young and old alike, he was, like the later and more celebrated Cliff Huxtable character on *The Cosby Show*, an obvious antidote to the "negative" stereotypes of black manhood which have permeated mainstream American culture for decades. By contributing my talents to the creation of this image of a humorous but sensitive, intelligent, and principled black man, especially within the context of such a highly visible show for a very young audience, it was clear that I would greatly enhance my record of socially progressive influence through my work. Also, as with those earlier chapters in my career, I had entered into a new family of collaborators whose mutual respect and commitment to shared ideals had come to mean much to me. Along with Jon Stone, Joan Ganz Cooney, Jim Henson, and the company's entire creative team, I would, through *Sesame Street*, be making a significant and lasting contribution to the educational enrichment of several generations of the world's children. For me, the choice between this and Tyrone was no choice at all.

Sesame Street cast photo with: Top L-R: Will Lee, Buster the Horse, Alaina Reed, Grover, and me. Middle L-R: Bob McGrath, Bert, Ernie, Oscar the Grouch, Loretta Long, Count Von Count, Rodeo Rosie, Biff, and Big Bird. Bottom L-R: Emilio Delgado, Ruby (?), Sonia Manzano, Northern Calloway, Prairie Dawn, Cookie Monster, and Linda Bove. 1979. (Courtesy of Sesame Workshop.)

CHAPTER SEVEN
Mastery

Soul Dreamer

Soul dreamer
Peace redeemer
Originating innovator
Reflection of the life creator
Inner peace will take you higher
Yours is all that you desire
Eject erect from broken chains
Architect of spirit planes
Plan your span of grandstand visions
Stand to hand down grand decisions

Soul dreamer
Peace redeemer
Regenerating instigator
Super funky gladiator
You are the night, the dark intruder
With the power of Chaka, Shango, and Buddha
You walk through fire like a cool summer breeze
Making demons and dictators fall to their knees
Hurricanes rumble deep in your lungs
Telling your tale in nine thousand tongues

Moon seducer
Mama Juicer
Copulating populator
Universal operator
Women faint, fall under a trance
When they catch a glance of your juju dance
Babies sleep by the sound of your song
For love is the music you wake with the dawn
And your rhythms ride on the winds of the East
For you are the soul dreamer, redeemer of peace.

6/11/74

To my good fortune and my great relief, the considerations which had led to my banishment from *All My Children* did not extend beyond the realm of daytime television. I could continue an arc of success in legitimate theater, which had become a vital source of creative fulfillment for me. The range and abundance of stage roles which have come my way over the last three decades have provided me with both another source of income and a respectable level of professional achievement. But even more importantly, this body of work has created a link between my own spiritual journey and that of my people, a connection which has been deeply resonant and meaningful to me. It has, indeed, been a lifeline to the pulse of all of humanity, which, particularly through the act of live performance, has sustained and enriched me far beyond any of the rewards of recognition or material success.

The first theater role to be offered me after joining the cast of *Sesame Street* came from actor-director Bill Duke. I had seen Bill perform a few years earlier in Gil Moses' strikingly original Broadway production of Melvin Van Peebles' *Ain't Supposed To Die a Natural Death*, which had also included strong work from Dick Williams, Gloria Edwards, Clebert Ford, Arthur French, Carl Gordon, Barbara Alston, Jimmy Hayeson, Albert Hall, and especially Garrett Morris (later of *Saturday Night Live* fame), whose rendition of "Lilly Did the Zampoo Oogy" was a showstopper. The play that Bill was directing was a political melodrama written by Garrett entitled *A Secret Place*, which was being presented by Ellen Stewart's La Mama Experimental Theatre Club on the Lower East Side where we ran it through the winter of '74 and '75. My part was that of Caesar Pittman, the fictitious young romantic hero of a modern urban revolution. Bill's direction was both mysterious and graphic with flashes of the brilliance which would be later exhibited by him in films such as *Deep Cover* and *Hoodlum*. There were also standout performances from

Me as Pretty Eddie in EVERY NIGHT WHEN THE SUN GOES DOWN with Marge Eliot, 1976. (Courtesy of Martha Holmes.)

Obba Babatunde, Akin Babatunde, Frank Adu, and a young (and skinny) Harvey Fierstein.

My next major acting project was another collaboration with Gil Moses, my first since *Willie Dynamite*. It was produced in 1976 by Wynn Handman's American Place Theatre, where I had recently staged Ed Bullins' *House Party*. The play was Philip Hayes Dean's *Every Night When the Sun Goes Down*, a vibrant depiction of character and place, set in 1950s Pontiac, Michigan. Under Gilbert's typically stylish and insightful direction, I had a wonderful time playing Pretty Eddie, a colorful and poignant variation on the pimp roles which I had, by now, come close to perfecting. I enjoyed the company of a stellar cast which included Dick Ward, Joe Seneca, Billie Allen, Norman Matlock, Frank Adu, Marki Bey, and especially Marge Eliot as Eddie's woman, Caldonia.

The play received mixed reviews but the critics were unanimous in their praise of my work, giving me some of my best notices to that date. My performance also captured the attention of talent agent Richard Astor, who had come to see his client Norman Matlock and approached me backstage after the show. He subsequently offered me a contract and thus began a relationship that would last for the next fifteen years. As an added bonus, my portrayal of Pretty Eddie brought me my first nomination for an AUDELCO Award as Best Featured Actor.

The production was marked, however, by one frightening incident. One night, as I was about to make an entrance during the play's second act, Dick Ward, the venerable and well-seasoned veteran of stage and screen (*Brubaker, Across 110th Street*) who was playing Clean Sam, the proprietor of the cheap hotel and bar that are the center of the play's activity, toppled forward. His fall broken by a table and chair on the set, he landed prone and face up at center stage. After several seconds of shock and confusion among company members and audience alike, the house lights went up. That famous phrase that is so often applied with humor was announced over the public address system, "Is there a doctor in the house?" With many in attendance apparently thinking that this might be a part of the play, valuable seconds passed before anyone responded. Eventually, a physician found his way from the audience to the stage and, with the help of a few others, resuscitated Mr. Ward, whose heart had actually stopped beating for a few moments. After the theater was emptied and Dick had been transported to nearby St. Clare's Hospital, we all gathered near his bedside with his wife and were assured by hospital staff that he would be all right. Dick's understudy, Hugh Hurd, completed the run, and Dick Ward lived for several more years before succumbing to another heart attack, this time fatally.

Within a year after *Every Night* came the second play of Richard Wesley's that I would premiere at the Manhattan Theatre Club, his searing, eloquent ode to the loss of young manhood, *The Last Street Play*. I was asked to play Frankie Sojourner, a former inner-city gang leader and lost soul. Along with three of his cronies and his ever loyal childhood sweetheart, he desperately, and tragically, clings to the memories of a glorified youth as he slowly but inevitably descends into a Dantesque inferno.

Tom Bullard, a young associate of Lynne Meadow's previously unknown to me or to Richard, was selected to direct the production. The play, however, was cast to utter perfection. Yvette Hawkins, my dear fellow New Lafayette alumnus, gave a heart-wrenching performance as Frankie's woman, Rita. Maurice Woods as Essex Braxton, Frankie's long-time rival, was mesmerizing and chilling. My fellow gang members, Eldridge, Tiny, and Lucky, were portrayed with brilliant humor and pathos by Richard Gant, Brent Jennings, and Herb Kerr. And last but not least, the role of Zeke, the aging wino who symbolized Frankie's bleak future, was masterfully performed by Morgan Freeman in the first of several collaborations I would enjoy with this consummate actor and future film star.

The play opened in May of 1977. The New York press bestowed uniform praise upon every aspect of the production, from Richard's script, to Tom's direction, to David Potts' sets, to Judy Dearing's costumes, and to each and every performance, without exception. Martin Gottfried of *The New York Post* called the play's climax "one of the most vivid and devastating theater moments I've ever experienced." This phenomenal critical success led to my first experience at being involved in a showcase production moving toward a commercial success. The Manhattan Theatre Club, as a not-for-profit institution, was in no position to produce the play on Broadway or even at a less costly Off-Broadway establishment. Eventually, a producer by the name of Lipton bought the option to move *The Last Street Play* to Broadway. I only recently discovered that the mysterious Mr. Lipton was none other than James Lipton, the famous head of The Actors Studio program at New York's New School and host of the renowned television show on the BRAVO Channel.

In his desire to make the piece more "accessible," Lipton felt the need to both re-conceive and re-stage the entire production. First of all, Tom Bullard, who happened to be white, was replaced as director by the Broadway and regional theater veteran Hal Scott, who was black. I knew Hal as one of the original cast members of *The Blacks* and also as a distant cousin of Bob Macbeth's. In spite of each of our stellar performances and reviews, Hal proceeded to audition each cast member anew, as well as other actors who were enthusiastically vying for the roles we had created.

This led, eventually, to the newly named *The Mighty Gents* (the name of Frankie's gang), musically scored, and partially recast. In the pivotal roles of Rita, Braxton, and Frankie, Yvette, Maurice, and I were replaced by the slightly younger and, presumably, more "commercially attractive" Starletta DuPois (ironically, a New Lafayette protégée), Howard Rollins, Jr., and Dorian Harewood, respectively. Morgan, Richard, Brent, and Herb went on to repeat their original roles. Morgan, deservedly, would win a Clarence Derwent Award as best featured actor for his performance on Broadway, but *The Mighty Gents* was roundly attacked by the New York critical establishment and closed within a few weeks of its opening, giving credence, once again, to the old axiom "If it ain't broke, don't fix it." Shocked and outraged by the insult we had been dealt, neither Maurice, Yvette, nor I could bring ourselves to see a performance of what we all considered to be a painful missed opportunity. It would be twelve years before I would reunite with both Richard Wesley and the Manhattan Theatre Club by playing the lead role in MTC's 1989 staging of Wesley's *The Talented Tenth*. Unfortunately, neither Yvette Hawkins nor Maurice Woods would live long enough to enjoy a similar reconciliation.

The summer of 1977 was highlighted by my first and only season at The Eugene O'Neill Theatre Conference in Waterford, Connecticut. The O'Neill Conference, founded and headed by Yale's Dean of Drama and legendary theater director, Lloyd Richards, is an annual gathering of selected theater artists and dramaturges. The purpose of the O'Neill is the exploration and development of new works by a collection of some of America's finest and most promising playwrights. The list of dramatists who have been nurtured by Richards and the scores of actors, directors, and critics who have been associated with the conference is a virtual Who's Who of contemporary theater. I felt extremely honored to be a part of this "summer camp with a purpose." I was particularly pleased to help inaugurate the television and film workshop which, for the first time in the conference's history, focused on the development of plays for the screen. I was assigned to perform in a new teledrama written by Negro Ensemble Company alumnus Gus Edwards, marking my first collaboration with fellow actors Gil Lewis, Michelle Shay, and Ted Ross. I had a wonderful time both working with and getting to know these three singularly talented individuals.

The following spring I was selected by director Oz Scott to play the part of Ike Hockenhull, the first husband of Mahalia Jackson, in Woodie King, Jr.'s New Federal Theatre production of Don Evans' musical bio-drama, *Mahalia*. Don was a client of Nasaba Artists' Management and a longtime friend, so it was a real pleasure to work on his homage to Gospel music's greatest singing star. This was my first chance to portray an actual person whose life I could research and attempt to authenticate on stage. We were also extremely fortunate to have the extraordinary Esther Marrow as Mahalia, a great Gospel star in her own right. Whatever Esther may have lacked in acting skills she more than made up for with her wondrous singing voice. It was sheer joy just to hear the choir accompany her powerful renditions of some of Jackson's most popular and memorable songs each night.

Among the cast we were blessed to have an abundance of notable talent, such as actors Frances Foster, Loretta Devine, and Chuck Patterson, dancers Otis Sallid, Al Perryman, and Mabel Robinson, singers William Hardy and Lee Cooper, and, in his delightful acting debut, for which he also played trumpet, the renowned jazz musician and bandleader, Nat Adderley. In addition, the production's original musical score was written by none other than John Lewis, founder and leader of the legendary Modern Jazz Quartet. The music was arranged and conducted by the great Luther Henderson. The supreme level of artistry embodied by this company inspired me to do my best within what was essentially a supporting role. In spite of this remarkable blending of talents under Scott's skillful direction and several good, if not spectacular reviews, the show's run ended after only four weeks at the Henry Street Playhouse. There were a few attempts

SESAME STREET float in Macy's Parade with Sonia, me, Will Lee, Loretta, Bob, Muppets, and kids, including Bob's Cathlin and my Rasheda, 1979. (Courtesy of Sesame Workshop.)

by others to revive this show some years later, most notably with Patti LaBelle starring as Mahalia in one short-lived production.

The summer of '78 was highlighted by the taping of CTW's first major prime-time special, *Christmas Eve on Sesame Street*, written and directed by Jon Stone. This charming production, which first aired during Christmas that year, has gone on to become a perennial holiday favorite in re-runs and video sales and rentals. With its simple tale of concern for our neighbors and the joys of giving, *Christmas Eve* represents, in my opinion, the very best example of the true spirit of *Sesame Street*. It and the later (1983) *Please Don't Eat the Pictures*, shot entirely within New York's Metropolitan Museum of Art, were specials in the truest sense of the word and will hopefully pass the test of time and continue to entertain and delight generations to come.

In addition to 1978 being a year of artistic stimulation and growth this was also a period of exceptional personal fulfillment and prosperity. Sharon and I were truly reveling in the joys of both marriage and parenthood with three-and-a-half-year-old Rasheda the light of our lives. Within a year our second daughter, Solana Joy, would be born and we would move from our New York City apartment to our first home in suburban New Jersey. Given the relatively limited financial compensation derived from public television, what made this financial growth and security possible was my good fortune in being introduced by Loretta Long ("Susan" on *Sesame Street)* to the American Program Bureau (APB) and the world of personal appearances. In the late seventies and throughout the eighties, before the advent of cable television and Nick Jr. invaded its territory, *Sesame Street* remained a uniquely successful phenomenon: a hip, funny, wholesome and remarkably educational program for the very young (and the not so young). Those of us appearing on the show who were able and willing to travel the countryside performing for hundreds of thousands of families who had come to know and love our characters were in great demand. With our short taping season, we could literally spend most of the year touring from coast to coast, including Canada, delighting scores of fans with songs and games from the show, or by simply showing up and signing autographs and shaking hands. Concert halls, shopping malls, state and county fairs, festivals, and theme parks became venues for these lovefests which would eventually surpass the TV show itself in their rewards to us, both spiritually and financially.

These opportunities to travel did, however, place somewhat of a burden upon my family life. Whenever possible, Sharon and I would put the kids in the car and we would all drive to my destination, turning these jobs into family excursions, or at other times we would deposit the kids with relatives and extend my assignment in some beautiful locale into a romantic getaway. But much of the time this was not feasible and the family bore the hardship of my absences. Obviously, what made all this acceptable was the financial reward. Within my first ten years of being on *Sesame Street*, initially through APB, and then with the newly formed and smaller speakers' bureau, Paul Jacob Productions, the steadily growing stream of bookings for concerts and personal appearances enabled me and other cast members to substantially enhance our incomes, especially during the heady times of the perceived economic boom of the Ronald Reagan presidential era. Numerous corporate, educational, and other community entities were eager to sponsor the kind of family entertainment that the *Sesame Street* cast members provided, leading some of us to erroneously believe that this kind of response would continue indefinitely.

The end of 1978 also provided me with another extraordinary opportunity within the New York theater scene. Joseph Papp, whose New York Shakespeare Festival had, over twenty years, become one of the premier arts institutions in the nation, especially in the interpretation of Shakespeare, decided to mount two Shakespearean productions using black and Hispanic actors exclusively. This was only an extension of an old tradition for Papp, who had a long history of giving actors such as James Earl Jones, Roscoe Lee Browne, Ruby Dee, Raul Julia, Ellen Holly, and others opportunities to play challenging roles in the classics. And, like American Place Theatre's Wynn Handman and Manhattan Theatre Club's Lynne Meadow, Joe was a white producer who had for years provided employment for New York's African-American acting community. Virtually every major black talent to emerge during the sixties and seventies had worked for either Handman, Meadow, or Papp, if not all three, as I had.

Joe, however, as the producer, promoter, and impresario responsible for such legendary successes as *Hair, That Championship Season, For Colored Girls Who Have Considered Suicide When the Rainbow Is Enuf, No Place To Be Somebody*, and *Chorus Line*, was in a class by himself.

My first experience working with Joe was for an experimental workshop production of a play written by Ruby Dee, entitled *Twin Bit Gardens*, which was rehearsed for several weeks during the spring of 1976 at the Festival's Public Theatre on Lafayette Street. Curiously, Papp insisted that Ruby direct her own play as well as perform the female lead ("Angel Annie"), a nearly impossible task even for someone as supremely gifted and experienced as she. With her equally renowned husband Ossie Davis as advisor and co-star ("Almight") along with me as the third lead ("Prophet") and an impressive string of supporting players that included Robert Christian, Arthur French, Cynthia Belgrave, Howard Rollins, Jr., Seret Scott, Bruce McGill, Maurice Copeland, and Rise Collins, to name a few, Ruby worked valiantly to pull this large and unwieldy piece together, only to have Joe suddenly terminate the project, after about three or four weeks of rehearsing and editing. He apologetically explained that, in spite of all our efforts, the piece had not come together sufficiently to warrant any further expense. The decision was a crushing disappointment to everyone, most especially to Ruby. Enjoyable as it was to work with these wonderful artists, this experience, and especially Joe's insistence on having Ruby direct her own play, raised some questions in my mind about the artistic vision and the true objectives of this complicated icon of American theater.

In any case, the two Shakespeare plays which Papp had chosen to mount, *Julius Caesar* and *Coriolanus*, were to be produced consecutively under the direction of Michael Langham and Wilford Leach, respectively, and then performed in rotation, repertory-style through the spring of 1979. Although cast entirely with black and Latino actors, there was no attempt by Papp or his directors to reset or otherwise adjust these plays to reflect the ethnicity of the company.

In my initial audition for Langham I used Frankie Sojourner's opening monologue in *The Last Street Play* and seemed to have struck him as an actor who could hold the stage alone. He asked that I repeat the

With Maurice Woods, Peter Francis James, Morgan Freeman, Peter Jay Fernandez, Count Stovall, Robert Christian, backstage at Public Theatre, 1979.

scene for Papp, who had, in fact, seen me in the original production the year before and had turned down an offer to move the show from MTC to the Public. I was selected by Joe and Michael to play the part of Brutus in *Caesar* and two smaller roles in *Coriolanus*. In spite of my questionable history with Joe, I recognized this as a wonderful career opportunity and was elated.

The company was an incredibly eclectic mixture of some of the best acting talents on the scene. It included, at one time or another, Gloria Foster, Morgan Freeman, Mary Alice, Robert Christian, Sonny Jim Gaines, Earl Hyman, Avery Brooks, Denzel Washington, Clarence Williams III, Michelle Shay, C.C.H. Pounder, Jaime Sanchez, Peter Francis James, Gylan Kain, Gil Lewis, Frankie Faison, Miriam Colon, Robbie McCauley, Arthur French, Clebert Ford, Maurice Woods, George Miles, Reginald Vel Johnson, Count Stovall, Peter J. Fernandez, Francisco Prado, Tucker Smallwood, William Jay, Clark Morgan, Norman Matlock, Frank Adu, and Leonard Jackson. It was, by far, the largest and most widely experienced company I had ever been a part of. Being chosen to play Brutus, who is, despite its title, the play's main protagonist and one of Shakespeare's more challenging roles, was both an honor and a humbling task. Fortunately for me, in the British-born Langham we had a veteran director renowned for his prolific work in the classics with the Royal Shakespeare Company and the National Theatre of Great Britain, and as head of the Tyrone Guthrie Theater in Minneapolis and the Stratford Festival in Canada. It was also brought to my attention that among his several interpretations of *Caesar* was one in which he directed the great Sir John Gielgud as Brutus, a fact that I found both extremely flattering and intimidating.

Not everyone in our acting company, however, shared in my appreciation of Langham. Clarence, who was slated to play Coriolanus, left the venture after only a few week's rehearsal, citing personal and artistic differences with Michael as the reason for his departure. Surprisingly, his wife, the remarkable Gloria Foster, stayed on to splendidly perform the role of Volumnia, mother to Coriolanus.

In addition, the extremely gifted but volatile Leonard Jackson, who had been perfectly cast as Caesar, chose the most public of moments to dramatically air his grievances with Langham. Joe had called a meeting for all to attend, in which vital company matters were to be addressed. As the gathering of the forty-plus actors began to assemble and come to attention, Leonard rose from his seat and slowly, menacingly approached the stage where Joe and Michael were seated. The room came to a hush as the compact, powerfully built Jackson moved deliberately toward the frail, elderly, chain-smoking British director and hissed "You low-life, racist bastard, I will rip your puny heart out with my bare hands." We were all struck dumb with shock. I had known Leonard for ten years, since we had performed together in *Electronic Nigger*, and knew that despite his famously hot temper, his bark was much bigger than his bite. (Years later I would make the mistake of recommending him for a role on *Sesame Street*, another job that he would sabotage within a few months). Sure enough, after threateningly coming within inches of Michael, who appeared to be close to cardiac arrest, he receded, turned, and calmly walked away, undoubtedly well aware that he had driven yet another nail into the coffin of a once promising career. Within a matter of days my old friend Sonny Jim Gaines, with whom I had shared the stage countless times during the days of New Lafayette, was chosen to replace Leonard as Caesar.

With Langham's guidance, I came to discover that the key to playing Brutus lay in his nobility of spirit and his unwavering commitment to what he perceived to be the right thing, despite the consequences, even if it meant killing his emperor and former father figure. With this arc of reality firmly set, the events within the play took on a momentum of inevitability which rang true from scene to scene as the audience followed Brutus on his heroically tragic spiritual trajectory. Having never previously performed a Shakespearean play, I found the sense of challenge, discovery and accomplishment inherent in this experience to be extremely exhilarating. The most powerful scenes, for me and audiences alike, were those between Brutus and Gylan Kain's Cassius (in spite of Gylan's unnerving but compelling unpredictability) and, especially, those between me and the perennially wonderful Mary Alice as my wife Portia.

My success with this role and, in fact, of the entire production was heralded by the largest array of both the New York and national press that I had ever experienced. In addition to all of the daily papers, *Time*, *Newsweek*, and *The New Yorker* magazines also ran extensive and largely favorable reviews. Of my performance, *The New Yorker*'s Edith Oliver wrote, *"Roscoe Orman's Brutus towers so far above all else that the production could almost be said to be lopsided – no one has the measure to become his antagonist in any scene, and rarely his equal. His Brutus has such virtue (honor, indeed, is the key to the performance), such candor and emotion that the character, for the first time in my experience, becomes a kind of romantic hero as well as a tragic one."* The sad irony is that such extreme praise, much as I tried to distance myself from it and be objective, infected my work with a self-satisfaction and complacency which, like an invisible bandit, robbed my performance of its sense of discovery, and over time its potential for exploration and growth. A tough lesson well learned. Fortunately, my work on the two smaller roles for *Coriolanus* which, with Morgan replacing Clarence as the title character, was more evenly performed by the entire company, offered me far less of a challenge and was, thus, easily sustained and improved upon over the entire run of that play.

In spite of these great successes, by far the highlight of 1979 was the birth of our second daughter Solana Joy on March 9th of that year. Sharon carried her for several weeks beyond her expected delivery date. The sense of anticipation among my family, including my fellow cast members, became nearly unbearable. When the daily query of "Has she had it yet?" was finally answered with a resounding "Yes," the feeling of relief and celebration throughout the company was palpable. Everyone, from Joe on down, became caught up in the joy of the moment, offering a variety of lovely gifts for the new baby. Ironically, two other company members, Frankie Faison and Avery Brooks, were both blessed with baby girls around the same time.

The birth of Solana also became the catalyst for another major change in our lives, namely, a move from New York City to the suburbs. With two young daughters to raise, it became obvious to both Sharon and me that it would be far less challenging and dangerous (and expensive) for us to live in a more tranquil suburban community than in the heart of Manhattan. So, in June of 1979, three months after Solana's birth, the four of us migrated across the Hudson to the environs of northern New Jersey and into our first single-family home.

My next stage assignment, although less daunting than the nearly six months of performing three Shakespearean roles, proved to be equally fulfilling and even more fun. Samm-Art Williams' play *The Sixteenth Round* was selected by Douglas Turner Ward to be the 1980 premiere production for the Negro Ensemble Company's new location at Theatre Four on West 55th Street. Samm had recently scored big with Ward's staging of *Home,* a three-character, semi-autobiographical play featuring Charles Brown, Michele Shay, and L. Scott Caldwell, which had been successfully transplanted to Broadway and honored with several Tony nominations.

For *Sixteenth Round* I was chosen to play the part of Lamar Jefferson, an ex-prizefighter turned hit-man for the underworld whom I envisioned as a sort of "angel of death." He is assigned by his bosses to kill an old rival and boxing stable-mate played by Paul Benjamin. Paul's character, a former heavyweight contender who'd fallen on hard times, was a noble but beaten figure kept alive primarily by the loving care and support of his strong and loyal woman played by Rosalind Cash. Unlike *Home*, this was a dark and brooding piece with flashes of beauty reflected in the oddly complex relationship of these three off-beat characters. This production also marked the directorial debut of Horacena Taylor, a veteran stage manager with NEC and a truly splendid individual.

Paul and Rosalind were two long-time West Coast residents whom I had known for many years but had never worked with. They were among those rare veterans of the "blaxploitation" film era who had, against strong odds, created a livelihood for themselves in Hollywood. Besides being extremely gracious and amiable human beings, both were wonderfully supportive and professional artists, and despite the lukewarm response to this unusual piece among the mainstream press, I found the experience of performing and becoming better acquainted with these good souls to be a pure and total delight.

Me with Rasheda at age 4, 1979.

Me with Solana at age 2, 1981.

Me, Pancho, Cookie, and Leslie, 1981.

Sharon with Miles at age 4, 1989.

Rasheda, Cheyenne, and Solana, 1994.

Sharon with Cheyenne at age 4, 1998.

Me, Miles, Sharon, Solana, and Cheyenne at Miles' high school graduation, 2003.

CHAPTER EIGHT
Maturation

POEM FOR WILLY

My friend, in this deep silence of sleep
Hear the thunderous applause of hearts
That sing for yours, a heart
That gave such joy, so well
For days unnumbered, in ways unmeasured
Sharing wisdom mixed with loving care
To form a special brew of teaching
With your generous laughter filled with hope
With your pain-filled voice raised against injustice
With those wond'rous glowing eyes approving
With a smiling nod
With your honesty, your warmth, your love.
The curtain now descends
Peace, be still, and rest
You've taught us well, dear friend
Our lives have so been blessed.

12/15/82

MAURICE

He was a gentle warrior
A singular voice
with a strength hushed
under the lush timbre that
rolled from a harbor deep
somewhere behind those smiling eyes
and gleaming teeth

A giant redwood of a man, private
unmistakably his own
With a penetrating wit and style
He moved with athletic grace and ease
through the corridors and byways of his time

With his friends he showed and shared himself
Evolving, moving with us
to make life whole and new and true

In the collective spirit of our art
He was one with us
And will be forever
This giant redwood named Maurice.

11/27/83

T*he Sixteenth Round* turned out to be the last performance of mine to be witnessed by two of my dearest colleagues. Will Lee, the veteran character actor, played the beloved Mr. Hooper on Sesame Street from the show's inception in 1969 until his death in 1982. Will was a man of extraordinary experience and generosity of spirit. Born and raised on New York's Lower East Side, he became a member of the legendary Group Theatre of the 1930s, which spawned some the most influential talents of the 20th century theater, including Lee Strasburg, Harold Clurman, Clifford Odets, Elia Kazan, and Morris Carnovsky, to name a few. Will was an actor and a teacher with an infectious passion for both the craft and the politics of theater. I first met him in the mid-sixties at a Queens College seminar on political theater to which several members of FST had been invited. I was immediately struck by the animated and fiery conviction of this diminutive figure. A decade later, when I joined him as a member of the Sesame Street family, I found him to be no less energetic in his commitment to art and society, and, to my delight, we instantly developed a mutual respect and friendship. I saw in Will a kindred spirit and we talked about a wide range of subjects over the next decade. I learned more about his political activist background, including his association with people like the great Paul Robeson and about his being blacklisted during the Joseph McCarthy witch hunts of the 1950s. I became an eager audience to his generous storytelling and I was especially appreciative of his insightful comments about my own work. Beginning with *The Last Street Play* until his passing, he witnessed nearly everything that I did on stage and I always looked forward to his candid and knowledgeable assessments of both the play and my performance, whether critical or complimentary. His death saddened many within the theater community as well as the legions of fans who had grown to love Mr. Hooper, the venerable storekeeper and friend to

Big Bird who always had a kind word and a warm smile. Will's passing also presented the Sesame Street team with its first experience of having to deal with what to do about the sudden disappearance of a long-standing member of its ensemble. The succession of Matt Robinson by Hal Miller and me in the role of Gordon were straightforward decisions made early enough in the show's existence to become merely brief ripples in its continuity. By contrast, Mr. Hooper, as the senior member of the cast and also the proprietor of the neighborhood's main hangout, had, over nearly 15 years, become a highly recognized fixture on Sesame Street, as central to the show's identity as Big Bird, Cookie Monster, or Bert and Ernie. Dulcie, Jon, and their production team had the option of either replacing Will with another actor (either as Mr. Hooper or as some other character after explaining Hooper's exit by his moving away from the neighborhood), or of actually honoring Will's passing by embracing it as an opportunity to confront the subject of the death of a loved one for our very young audience and their families. To their credit, they chose the latter, more courageous path.

Head writer Norman Stiles was assigned the task of composing a script to tackle this extremely sensitive subject in a way that was honest, informative, and yet non-threatening and uplifting. Norman met the challenge brilliantly. With touches of humor, wisdom, and deep feeling, the script allowed each cast member, in explaining the meaning of Mr. Hooper's death to a stunned and uncomprehending Big Bird, to candidly share our own real sense of grief over the loss of our beloved friend and colleague. The show premiered on Thanksgiving Day of 1983 to allow as many family members as possible to experience it together, capturing, in the process, a record high share of the viewing audience. To this day, it remains one of the proudest and most honored moments in *Sesame Street*'s history.

Within less than a year of Will's death, another dear friend and theater colleague, Maurice Woods, passed prematurely after spending several months bravely battling an undisclosed illness. Maurice was a native of Chicago who, until his early thirties, had lived there working his way up as a successful corporate executive for the Seagrams Company before deciding to follow his lifelong dream of becoming an actor.

Moving to New York, he embarked upon his new career with a determination and maturity which soon began to establish him as one of the more serious among the city's thriving community of actors. Although formally unacquainted, during '74 and '75 we would occasionally cross paths at auditions or other functions. Then, one early summer day in 1975, as Sharon and I pushed Rasheda's stroller through Central Park, we encountered another couple also pushing a baby's stroller, and, although we didn't actually know each other by name, Maurice and I both recognized each other, stopped to introduce ourselves, our wives, and our babies, and thus began a friendship which lasted until his untimely death in 1983.

Shortly after our meeting in the park we had the experience of working together in *The Last Street Play* and immediately began to develop a mutual respect and admiration, both as artists and as men, which enhanced our already burgeoning friendship. Our chemistry on-stage, much like that between Morgan Freeman and me in this production and others, became one of the many highlights of my career during this wonderful period. Maurice and I worked together only once again, in the Shakespeare plays, but in early '83 he convinced me to accept an offer to play the lead role in The Riverside Church's production of *Breaking Light*, Marcus Hemphill's saga about the legend of John Henry, under Morgan's direction. I needed convincing only because the role was so large and the pay so little, but within the first few days of rehearsal I was glad that I had accepted. Morgan proved to be an exceptionally gifted director, which should not have been surprising, given his extraordinary talent, intelligence, and persuasive personality.

Maurice, who, at a few inches taller and thirty pounds heavier than I, would have been a more natural choice for the gargantuan John Henry, had passed on this role to take advantage of a more lucrative offer to co-star with Robert Conrad in a made-for-TV movie about Watergate conspirator G. Gordon Liddy. The role of John Henry, however, proved to be a most enjoyable challenge in which I had the task of not only enhancing my muscular appearance but of aging from seventeen to forty-two years old. With the aid of an excellent hairpiece and a clean shaven face, I was so fully convincing in the play's earlier scenes that virtually no one in the audience, including some long-time friends, recognized the actor playing the strapping young John Henry. It wasn't until later, when I added a fake mustache for the character's middle-age years, that some of them began to realize that it had been me all along. Morgan had also cast the majority of the play's characters with actors who were noticeably smaller than myself, thereby giving the impression of my being larger than my actual six feet and 190 pounds. In addition to Morgan, I also had the pleasure of working again with such colleagues as Clebert Ford, Arthur French, Chuck Patterson, Neal Harris, and close friend and confidant Tommy Hicks, as well as for the first time with Elden Bullock, Noble Lee Lester, Mel Boudraux, Barbara Clarke, Lori Hayes, and the multi-talented Phyllis Yvonne Stickney. Although not reviewed by the press, this family-friendly saga enjoyed an enthusiastic response from Riverside's loyal audience and many others, including three-year-old Solana Joy Orman. I am forever indebted to my dearly departed friend and colleague Maurice for this memorable gift.

Another long-time friend, Sonny Jim Gaines, provided me with my next theatrical success in the New Federal Theatre's 1984 production of his play, *Twenty Year Friends*. Gaines had made an indelible mark as the most powerful presence within New Lafayette's acting company with such roles as Cliff Dawson in *In the Wine Time*, O.D. Best in *The Duplex*, Harrison Baines in *We Righteous Bombers*, Curt in *Goin'a Buffalo*, and his Obie Award–winning performance as Bill Horton in *The Fabulous Miss Marie*. As a younger actor, I benefited immeasurably from the experience of playing opposite this complex, charismatic, and imposing figure in a string of productions over five years. Towards the end of New Lafayette's existence, however, he began to also make his mark as a gifted playwright with the company's productions of his deceptively simple but insightful dramas *A Hard Head Makes a Soft Behind* and *What If It Had Turned Up Heads?* A few years prior to this he had scored successfully with his first play *Don't Let It Go to Your Head* at the New Federal, in which I first saw actors Herb Kerr, Mel Winkler, Peggy Kilpatrick, and a young Phylicia Ayers-Allen. *Friends*, however, was, in my opinion, Gaines' most accomplished and well-rounded piece. As the title suggests, it concerns the relationships among a group of long-time friends, three married couples, all of whom rally to the support of the one among them who is experiencing a severe mid-life crisis. My performance as Money, the middle-aged, worldly-wise pimp with a heart of gold was my first experience at playing one of Gaines' full-bodied, mature, and finely crafted portraitures and was certainly the most complex and compelling version of this character-type in my repertoire. Displaying a strong and sensitive hand at directing, Andre Mtumi assembled a truly wonderful cast which included Louise Stubbs, Neal Harris, Clebert Ford, Juanita Clark, and Joyce Walker, with whom I hadn't worked since our co-starring together in *Willie Dynamite* some ten years earlier. Every one of the forty-plus performances of Sonny Jim's splendid homage to friendship and commitment was a joyously heartfelt expression of love in which each performer had ample opportunity to shine. Our audiences responded enthusiastically and, as an added treat, Vivian Robinson and the AUDELCO Awards committee honored me with my second award nomination for my work in this play.

CHAPTER NINE
Sesame Kaleidoscope

A Little Poem

Can you write a little poem
That sings pitter patter melodies?
A poem with a smile
To make spirits blend with the bending breeze?
Can the rain fall through your poem
And yet not wet the boat?
Is it light enough to pierce through stone,
So heavy it can float?
Is your poem on a page
And in the air like breath?
Will your poem live forever
And die with every death?
Is your poem always lonely
Yet everybody's friend?
Can you write a little poem
That does not have an end?

10/12/74

The continuing presence of *Sesame Street* in my life during the 1970s, '80s, and '90s along with my increasing identification with the show and the character of Gordon over these decades has effectively colored every aspect of my existence, professionally, personally, politically, economically, and otherwise. Some of the challenges associated with this recognition became unwelcome intrusions. Certainly, the requisite loss of anonymity attached to any sustained visibility within the "media" can be an annoyance. I have chosen, however, to accept this reality as a small price to pay for the rare privilege of earning a livelihood at doing something that I truly love. I am one of those performers who will only rarely refuse to sign an autograph or take a picture with a fan. Perhaps inspired by the fifty-year-old memory of having met Roy, Dale, Gabby, and Trigger or just simply to acknowledge and show appreciation for the acceptance and approval that we all, performers and non-performers alike, thrive upon, I have spent countless hours signing, posing, meeting, and greeting with thousands of *Sesame Street* fans, particularly the children. There is little doubt that for decades to come countless instances of connection between me and my young admirers will be memorialized by them as significant moments in their lives, just as I have done with Roy and company. I have been especially touched and inspired by my visits with children suffering from catastrophic, sometimes terminal illnesses or injuries at hospitals, special events, camps, or just randomly at general audience gatherings. These innocent victims of severe misfortune repeatedly exude an enormous sense of courage and wisdom beyond their years which leaves me feeling deeply privileged to have met them.

Another, less positive by-product of my association with the show has been the limited perspective and limiting effect of those within the industry who either offer or deny opportunities based upon their narrowly framed vision. Such challenges and stigmas attached to series television work have caused many actors to reject this type of "stability" in favor of more risk and flexibility in their careers. This choice may or may not lead to more and better opportunities. In my case, despite such pressures and the temptation to "move on to bigger and better things," the advantages associated with my job seemed to far outweigh the disadvantages. There was, of course, the obvious sense of fulfillment derived from providing such a positive impact upon our viewers and sharing a strong sense of fellowship and fun with co-workers. Over these three decades I have established a special brand of camaraderie with Bob, Loretta, Emilio, Sonia, Linda, Alan Muraoka, Desiree Casado, Olamide Faison, puppeteers Caroll, Kevin, Jerry Nelson, Richard Hunt, Frank Oz, Fran Brill, Pam Arciero, Marty Robinson, Joey Mazzarino, Carmen Osbahr, Dave Rudman, Stephanie D'Abruzzo, and Matt Vogel, as well as with other members of our extensive family of collaborators such as writers Jeff Moss, Sam Pottle, Joe Raposo, Chris Cerf, Emily Kingsley, Tony Geiss, and Judy Freudberg, directors Lisa Simon, Ted May, Emily Squires, Victor DiNapoli, Ken Diego, and Jim Martin, and production workers Chester "Chet" O'Brien, Mortimer "Snooky" O'Brien, Frankie Biondo, Blake Norton, Gordon Price, and others. These relationships, although perhaps rivaled in their longevity and their depth by my many associations within the world of theater, are unequaled in their continuity and breadth of recognition.

The early formative years of my association with the show were filled with solidifying moments of group camaraderie. Location shooting sessions were commonplace, taking us from local settings in and around New York City to more remote areas in places such as Taos, New Mexico, San Juan, Puerto Rico, or Toronto, Canada. Working on location and discovering new cultures together, always a stimulating bonding experience for a group of artists, was especially memorable and meaningful for a company like ours which has been in the process of accumulating years and even decades of professional and personal attachment to each other.

And what other job could have allowed me to share my life's work with my own children in a way so beneficial to both them and me? Beginning with Rasheda, who made her debut on the show in 1977 at the age of two and a half by singing the alphabet song with Ray Charles, all four have had their times of hanging out with Dad and his *Sesame Street* friends. Solana made her first appearance on the show when she and Keisha Knight Pulliam (before becoming Rudy on *The Cosby Show*), both three years old, sat on the steps with me as I read them a funny story about one of my favorite Muppet characters, Richard Hunt's Forgetful Jones. My son Miles, as I will describe in a later chapter, would have the most lasting and meaningful connection to the *Sesame* family, one that would add a significant dimension to his life's biography. And finally, there was Cheyenne, the youngest and probably the most artistically inclined of the four, who didn't make her first appearance on the show until the age of five but would bring the most joyous enthusiasm, self-awareness, and sense of excitement to each of these opportunities. For me and Sharon, all of these moments have provided memories which are priceless.

In addition to all of the above, where else could I have had the chance to work with and get to know the wide array of personalities who have graced the set of *Sesame Street* over the years? Imagine the thrill of sharing scenes or just playing host to the likes of Jose Ferrer, James Earl Jones, Lily Tomlin, Tracy Ullman, Denzel Washington, Gregory Hines, Julianne Moore, Mandy Patinkin, Harry Belafonte, Maya Angelou, John Candy, B.B. King, Itzhak Perlman, Whoopi Goldberg, Cheech Marin, Susan Sarandon, Stevie Wonder, Patti LaBelle, Ray Charles, Gladys Knight, Rosemary Clooney, Alicia Keys, Robert Townsend, Diana Ross, The Neville Brothers, Glenn Close, Alice Walker, Kathleen Turner, Liam Neeson, Spike Lee, Bobby McFerrin, Julius Erving, Joe Williams, George Benson, Dizzy Gillespie, Max Roach, Tito Puente, James Moody, Wynton and Branford Marsalis, Tony Bennett, Rosie O'Donnell, Hillary Rodham Clinton, Pat Nixon, Barbara Bush, Phil Donahue, and the list goes on and on. Just the experience of having shared so many special moments with people of this caliber would alone be reason for many to remain with *Sesame Street*.

My separate encounters with each of the above mentioned First Ladies provided me with an especially rare view of the contrasting personalities of these three women and how differently they had inhabited the same position of influence. The first such visit that I helped to host was that of Mrs. Nixon sometime in the early eighties, several years after the Watergate debacle and her husband's historic resignation and fall from grace.

I arrived at work that late January morning with no prior knowledge of the impending visit. As I entered the door to the studio on West Eighty-first Street I was surprised and intrigued to see the burly, well-groomed, and dark-suited man who greeted me with a nod and a smile of recognition. I had no idea who he might be until I noticed the wire trailing from the receiver in his ear to the inside of his suit jacket, a dead giveaway that he was Secret Service. But who was he here to protect? No sooner had the question entered my mind than I was approached by Dulcie to inform me that Pat Nixon and daughter Tricia and her two small children had come by to observe some of the day's taping. I was immediately escorted to the set where they were waiting and introduced. Both ladies seemed genuinely pleased to see me, and the two children were in obvious awe of their surroundings. The entire place seemed to be teeming with Secret Servicemen as I headed to wardrobe and makeup to prepare for the day's work.

The entire cast for that day's show was comprised of Caroll (as Big Bird) and me. I'm sure it was no accident, for security purposes, that the visit had been scheduled on a day when as few people as possible would be present and also on a day that would include the Bird, who was a family favorite. My inclusion in the event appeared to be pure luck. And what luck it was! Mrs. Nixon turned out to be among the most delightfully down-to-earth of guests I have ever hosted on our set. Between taping segments or when Caroll was doing solo shots, the former First Lady and I sat at a table in the arbor of the playground as her daughter and grandchildren explored Oscar's trashcan or Big Bird's nest. We chatted about a number of things, mostly about the joys of parenthood and grandparenthood.

The plain-looking face and shy demeanor of the woman before me betrayed the rigors of her storied life: her and her husband's decades-long ascendancy to the heights of power abruptly terminated in shame and infamy. It made her sense of grace and humility all the more admirable. Our unaffectedly amiable one-on-one moment of shared reflection was easily among the most serendipitous of my *Sesame Street* encounters and one that I have come to cherish. The fact that Richard Nixon and his presidency had been such an anathema to me and so many others of my generation made this surprising rendezvous all the more poignant.

Then, as an equally memorable addendum to the event, about two weeks later I received, unexpectedly, a bulky, heavily padded package at my home. After laboriously tearing off the wrapping, I was stunned to discover a copy of *The Memoirs of Richard Nixon* personally inscribed as follows, "*To Roscoe Orman, with appreciation for his contribution to Sesame Street, Richard Nixon, 2-9-81.*"

My second First Lady close encounter, with Mrs. Barbara Bush, was in sharp contrast to the above. Unlike the Nixons' casual visit, Mrs. Bush's foray into children's television was part of a large and heavily publicized campaign on her part to promote literacy among the nation's children and was to include a segment on the show with her reading to a group of pre-schoolers. What better venue to advance and serve such an effort than on America's most popular and respected children's television program! Scheduled, planned for, and widely announced months before her arrival, it came replete with not only Secret Service but an equally strong contingent of the media coordinated by our then head publicist Fran Kaufman.

Again I was greeted at the studio door (by then we had moved farther downtown to a facility on West Fifty-fifth Street), this time by not one but several Secret Servicemen. I gradually worked my way through the buzzing soundstage to the makeup room where Mrs. Bush was expected to arrive any minute. Within seconds she appeared at the entrance to the room and, upon seeing me, darted straight toward me with her hands extended. I wasn't sure if was about to be hugged, kissed, shaken, or otherwise greeted by the First Lady but braced myself for whatever might occur. I was, nevertheless, completely unprepared for what followed. Reaching up toward my face as if she were about to caress my cheeks, she proceeded to grab my bald pate and rub it as if it were a crystal ball as she proclaimed, "You have the perfect head."

Now, how does one respond when the grandmotherly wife of a sitting president grabs and rubs your head in a roomful of your fellow workers and a phalanx of armed and highly trained security personnel?

Had I been white I would have turned several shades of red. But given the history of young black boys having their heads rubbed by Southern bigots as both a gesture of condescension and a plea for good luck, I had more than just cause to take offense. However, given the situation and Mrs. Bush's well-earned reputation as the bawdy, good-natured, and lovable, albeit arrogant and dominating matriarch of a family that would nurture two presidents, better judgment told me to swallow my pride and feign flattery. As it were, I assumed a sheepish grin and muttered something akin to "Thanks," and acted like I meant it.

The next of my First Lady encounters was with Hillary Rodham Clinton, a woman who would, during her husband's two terms in office, drastically redefine the role of wife to the Commander-in-Chief. Her short-lived efforts to revolutionize the country's health care system during their first term transformed her into a political lightning rod, hero to some and pariah to others. Her much publicized visit to *Sesame Street* to promote nutrition and good eating habits for kids occurred during the second year of the Bill Clinton administration. By this time we had migrated to yet another taping facility at Kaufman Studios in Astoria, Queens. The sense of excitement surrounding her visit surpassed that of Mrs. Bush or, for that matter, of any other guest that I can remember. I'm sure that much of this feeling was generated by the sense of alignment that many of us connected with the show, including myself, had developed in regards to her husband's recent ascendancy and his policy goals in general. I would again meet Mrs. Clinton the following year,

Cast with Hillary Rodham Clinton. Alison Bartlett O'Reilly, Rosita, and Carmen Osbahr. Middle L-R: Big Bird, Peter Linz, Lisa Buckley, Angel Jemott, me, Loretta Long, Ruth Buzzi, and Emilio Delgado. Bottom L-R: Fran Brill, Annette Calud, Hillary Rodham Clinton, Linda Bove, and Sonia Manzano. (Courtesy of Sesame Workshop.)

this time with the President at the White House as a performer during the annual Easter Egg Hunt, an event which, as I came to discover, is much larger and more widely attended than I had ever imagined.

In neither of my two encounters with Mrs. Clinton, however, did I experience anything even vaguely resembling the kind of personal moment of connection (for better or worse) that I had with Mrs. Nixon or Mrs. Bush. My basic impression of her on both occasions was that of a supremely self-possessed individual who would never display either the idiosyncratic behavior of a Barbara Bush or the unguarded vulnerability of a Pat Nixon. Instead, I saw a reserved but straightforward and highly competent, no-nonsense woman who was truly a force to be reckoned with, qualities which much of America has since come to recognize and associate with United States Senator Hillary Rodham Clinton.

Another great benefit for all of us cast members has been the pleasure and privilege of traveling to virtually every corner of the United States and beyond serving as sort of unofficial goodwill ambassadors. In the process, we have absorbed the tremendous spirit that resides within the people of the United States, Canada, and the Caribbean Islands in a way that very few have had the opportunity to do. As Joan Cooney has said, *Sesame Street*, which is seen in over 140 countries, is the longest street in the world, upon which the sun never sets. The respect and admiration of literally millions of people from virtually every corner of the world who have been touched by *Sesame Street*'s long arm of imagination, love, and intelligence has become a powerful and compelling part of each of our lives.

These sentiments among our vast audience have been expressed in a multitude of ways. One of the more humorous examples of mine occurred in Canada during the mid-1980s. While doing a promotional appearance at a shopping center in West Edmonton, Ontario, I was warned by the mall's marketing director that I would be receiving a visit after my show from a group of college-aged kids who were exceptionally avid fans of *Sesame Street* and particularly of Gordon. I was told that this group was mostly members of an improvisational comedy team which had begun to make a name for itself around the West Edmonton area, at which point, I was shown a newspaper ad for one of their recent appearances at a local comedy club. Imagine my surprise when I looked down at the page and saw the ad which read "Appearing tonight, *Gordon's Big Bald Head.*" Gordon's Big Bald Head? Was this a joke? Apparently it wasn't. I was informed that, in fact, the young performers' naming of their group after me and my head was intended as a form of high praise. Upon meeting the troupe after my show, I was immediately convinced that this was the case. The look on each of their faces as they gathered around me to take pictures reflected a genuine sense of awe and admiration which could not have been faked. I had begun to discover even prior to this visit, especially in the provinces of Canada, that many of the former young fans of *Sesame Street* who were now in their late teens and early twenties felt, and were willing to express, the sweetest sense of adulation for us adult cast members who had been among their first teachers and role models and who now held a special place in their hearts even if, as in this case, the form of this expression may have been a bit unorthodox.

The simultaneous maturation of *Sesame Street* and of those of us who have inhabited its domain for three decades has created a living legacy which has evolved and expanded certainly beyond anyone's expectations and has built an immense reservoir of memory and goodwill within the collective consciousness of a national and global audience. My long association with the show has, accordingly, given me the privilege of serving the needs of children in a variety of capacities which have brought me great pride. In 1983 I was honored to be the keynote speaker (my first such assignment) at the Tenth Annual Advisory Board Dinner of the Kansas City, Missouri, Black Adoption Services League. More recently I performed this same function for the 2001 National Organization of Jewish Women's *Dare to Care* Fundraising Dinner in New Orleans (which reunited me with old friend John O'Neal) and also for The Coalition for Greater Cleveland's Children's 2002 *Voter Education Forum*. I hosted 1991's *Children's Lifeline Telethon,* which was taped in Nashville, Tennessee, and broadcast across various regions of the United States and Canada to raise national awareness of the hidden epidemic of child abuse. In both 1996 and '97 I had the pleasure of hosting and performing for the Children's Defense Fund's *Stand for Children* event in New York City, working shoulder-to-shoulder with CDF's legendary founder and guiding light, Marian Wright Edelman, whose passionate and energetic commitment to political and social change, particularly for the benefit of our children, had obviously not diminished since her early years of serving alongside Dr. King and the SCLC. (In our reminiscing about the movement days, Marian recommended a book which had recently been written by our dear mutual friend Tom Dent entitled *Southern Journey* in which Tom, some thirty years later, revisits many of the towns in the Deep South which had provided important turning points in the struggle for civil rights. It was while reading this book during the summer of '98 and contemplating a phone call or letter to Tom to congratulate him on this remarkable achievement that, sadly, I heard the news of his death.)

I went on to perform a role similar to my *Stand for Children* assignment for three years at the New York Port Authority's *New York City KidsDay* at the World Trade Center (the last one just a few months prior to the tragedy of 9/11/01). I resumed my post as emcee of this event in 2003 and each year since at New York's South Street Seaport. Back in 1996 I hosted the New Jersey portion of PBS's National *Act Against Violence* campaign, designed to recruit volunteers for organizations which assist young people in finding alternatives to crime, drugs, and violence.

The most recent of these opportunities to serve the needs of children has been my inclusion as part of the national cast of the Variety Club Telethon in Buffalo, New York, in 2003, 2004, and 2005. For forty years a carefully selected assortment of performers from across the country has attended this annual event in which they join with the various communities of Northwestern New

Hosting New York City KidsDay at World Trade Plaza, 2001.

York State to support the efforts of a number of children's charities, most notably the Children's Hospital of Buffalo. The tremendous outpouring of love and the long hours of tireless commitment exhibited by the diverse, mostly working class folk of this area were an absolute inspiration to me and each of the other entertainers, such as cooking guru Art "Mr. Food" Ginsburg, Jon "Bowser" Bauman of Sha Na Na, and Buffalo natives boxer "Baby" Joe Mesi, veteran singer Marlene Ricci, and the talented jazz quartet RichBlend. Such assignments as these performed in service to our children have brought me a sense of honor and fulfillment which I never would have imagined prior to *Sesame Street*.

There was one particularly memorable moment which for me stands out as a powerful example of the service provided by the work we do on *Sesame Street*. Sometime in the mid-1980s I performed my "Gordon" show before a large audience at a local college auditorium in Topeka, Kansas, under the auspices of the area's PBS-TV affiliate. My performance that day was highlighted by what began as a casual invitation halfway through the show for a few kids from the audience to come forward and join me but which unexpectedly led to a gradual but irreversible invasion of the stage by every single child in the 500-plus seat theater. After a few feeble attempts to stem the rushing tide, I finally surrendered and accepted this new configuration as part of the event, in the process learning a valuable lesson. Never again would I extend such a tempting invitation to an audience of preschoolers.

During the customary meet-and-greet session after the show, a chair was positioned outside of the theater, allowing for a long single-file line of children and their accompanying adults to approach me one by one. Despite its size and enthusiasm, the crowd was patient, polite, and appreciative in the warm and pleasant afternoon sun. About midway through the line, a young girl of approximately seven or eight years of age slowly approached me, her mother moving rather apprehensively alongside the wall facing my chair. Although the woman's quiet anxiety had caught my attention, I was totally unprepared for what followed.

As the girl reached me, her arms opened for a hug (one of the frequent and most enviable rewards I receive for my work) and, without saying a word, wrapped her little arms around my neck. I couldn't help but notice the unusually ardent, almost desperate quality of her embrace, and as I looked up to see her mother's reaction to this scene, tears were streaming down her emotion-filled face as she uncontrollably, but silently, sobbed. After what seemed like much longer than the several seconds that had actually transpired, the child released me, I composed myself to ask her name, she told me, I handed her an autographed photo, and the procession continued. When the last person on line had finally been greeted and I began to wrap up my visit, I saw the mother walking toward me, her tears now subsided and her hand extended to grab mine. In the course of expressing her gratitude, she explained that her daughter had been sexually abused by a family member some time ago and that I was actually the first adult male that she had been either able or willing to approach since the incident had taken place. As I looked into this mother's eyes, I held back my own tears and knew that the humbling effect of this encounter would stay with me for a very long time. I also knew that there were countless other families and individuals around the globe whose needs had been and would continue to be met by *Sesame Street* in ways that none of us will ever fully know. This had become just another part of our unique job description. All the fame, fortune, and artistic fulfillment in the world could not begin to compete with the honor and distinction of such service.

But just so as not to hold myself in too high esteem or place myself upon a pedestal, life has periodically and emphatically reminded me to remain humble, despite the occasional temptation to do otherwise. One of the more humorous examples of such a return to reality occurred in Indianapolis, Indiana, sometime during the early eighties. I was in town for a week-long appearance at the city's renowned children's museum, a model institution of its type which had a long history of enriching the intellectual and cultural lives of millions of its visitors, both young and old alike. I had a wonderful time performing for scores of the region's schoolchildren in the museum's nicely appointed theater and lecture hall.

One afternoon between performances, I retreated to a familiar nearby restaurant for a quiet lunch alone. I sat not far from the entrance directly across from another table where a neatly dressed middle-aged woman also sat alone, already enjoying her meal.

Soon after I had been seated, I noticed a man and a woman coming toward me on their way out of the restaurant. "Gordon!" the woman exclaimed, "How are you? We heard that you were appearing in town. Our entire family are such fans of yours and have enjoyed you for years." The beaming couple extended their hands to greet me, apologized for interrupting my solitude, and proceeded toward the door. Shortly afterward, as I began to eat my salad, another small party of customers approached. "Gordon, is that you? Oh, my God!" one of them shrieked. "We don't mean to interrupt your lunch, but it's so wonderful to see you." Throughout both of these exchanges the woman seated across from me looked up from her meal repeatedly with a look of delighted curiosity emblazoned upon her face as if to be asking herself, "Who is this man? And do I know him?" By the time that the third and the fourth persons had greeted me with expressions of familiarity and appreciation, the woman was visibly struggling to contain herself. As she went on to finish her meal, she stole furtive glances at me, smiling, almost blushing with embarrassment.

Finally, after paying her bill, she came over to my table before leaving, presumably I thought, to ask who I was. Instead, she began, "Excuse me Gordon, but I just had to tell you how thrilled I am to see you too. I also enjoy your work." Somewhat surprised, I thanked her. She continued, "By the way, I hear that you will be performing soon in my hometown of Buffalo." I thought for a second, then replied, "No, I'm afraid you are mistaken."

"But," she insisted, "I'm certain that I read about your upcoming appearance there in our local newspaper." I assured her that I absolutely, positively had no plans to be in Buffalo anytime soon. The look on her face was a cross between utter befuddlement and disappointment as she asked with profound sincerity, "But…you are Gordon Lightfoot, aren't you?"

In addition to being a reality check, that story has come to symbolize, for me, the absurd nature of fame and the stupidity that so many of us are susceptible to when in close proximity to even mistaken celebrity.

Me performing an annual Christmas show in St. Croix, Virgin Islands, 1983.

Preparing to shoot scene with Sonia, Loretta, and Jon Stone in foreground, 1981.

Publicist Fran Kaufman, First Lady Barbara Bush, muppeteer Camille Kampouris, and me on the set, 1989.

Miles, Loretta, Big Bird, and me with NYC Mayor David Dinkins, 1991. (Courtesy of Sesame Workshop.)

Me and Oscar doing a scene with Denzel Washington, 1989. (Courtesy of Sesame Workshop.)

Kevin Clash, Elmo, and me with friends Jacob and Caleb Taylor. (Courtesy of Wanda Witherspoon.)

CHAPTER TEN
Middle Passage

TEMPUS (FOR THE DUKE)

And now
We are here
In time
To be possessed by our own countenance
Once again
Removed from the vagrant rogues
Who stalk our bones and hollow eyes
As we see the unfolding veils of innocence molding
Into vision.
Personified, we are here
Now graced
To embrace our harvest in the moonlight
Gazing over scattered brains
Gone gray and crazy
With their age-drawn longing
For time.
The journey precedes us in the wilderness
And we move on
Collecting the primal rhythm
Of our dreams, you
Reflecting the quest in me
Ingrained by ancestral fields
Not yet flourished
But sown strong by the enduring hands
Of time
Flexed and stretched across our skulls
Like the wind-swept rain on the horizon.
We are here
On this shattered glass terrain
To gather within us our reservoir
Of time.

5/27/74

In 1949, when George Orwell's terrifying political satire about the year *1984* was first published, it set into motion a collective sense of foreboding within the national and global psyche. As this infamous year of "Big Brother" approached, the media, as it is wont to do, thrived upon its own inflation of this phenomenon. Personally, I did feel, along with millions of others, I'm sure, the subliminally suggestive influence of Orwell's prescience as 1984 unfolded. At year's end I was certain that it had, in some respects, lived up to his prophesy. For me, the interplay between the joys and the sorrows as well as the sheer magnitude of the year's key events in both my personal and professional lives set 1984 apart, marking it as a major turning point in my journey.

The year, as a whole my most prosperous to date, afforded me an unprecedented sense of comfort and mobility, and, in addition to this foundation of financial abundance, Sharon and I were, early in the year, blessed with the conception of our son, Miles. Through amniocentesis, we opted to know the gender of our third child and were delighted to discover that our daughters, nine-year-old Rasheda and five-year-old Solana, would have a baby brother at year's end. Within weeks of this joyous news, however, we also learned that my father, who was now living in Los Angeles, had been diagnosed with lung cancer. He lived not far from my Aunt Cora. I had briefly visited him there a few years before. He would probably not survive through the year. I had seen my father only three or four times during my entire childhood and adolescence and those meetings were always tinged with an underlying sadness and a sense of loss. Surprisingly, we were reunited in my adulthood, during the last years of New Lafayette, when he discovered my name in a newspaper ad for my Fillmore East production of *How Do You Do*. He wrote me, asking that we meet. In the intervening years, we would develop a friendship based, presumably, upon his respect and pride for what I had accomplished in life and also upon my own growing appreciation for his innate goodness, intelligence, and charm, despite his glaring flaws and failures, and also a powerful desire, on my part, to know, understand, and, perhaps, even help him on his life's journey.

It was decided that the family would drive to Los Angeles in early July, spend a few weeks visiting my father and Aunt Cora and tour the West Coast. We planned to drive back to New Jersey at month's end. I had once before, under very different circumstances and with a humorous turn of events, made the three-thousand mile drive between coasts. It was during the summer of '73, when Whitman Mayo, who at the time had temporarily retired from acting in order to serve as my agent and personal manager, joined me for a high-speed three-day trip to L.A. so that we might pursue my shot at fame on the heels of *Willie Dynamite*. Upon our arrival, we received word that the casting people at NBC-TV had been trying to reach Whit to audition him for an upcoming guest appearance on *Sanford and Son*. Without even unpacking our bags, we headed for NBC where Whit tried to convince anyone who would listen that they should consider me for the role instead of him. But they would have none of it; it was he they were interested in for the part of Redd Foxx's friend and neighbor Grady. Finally, Whit agreed to be considered for the job and was hired. He was so impressive as Grady that he was asked to sign on as a regular cast member, eventually filling in for a whole season during which Foxx held out for a better contract. After a few seasons, there was a spin-off into his own short-lived series entitled *Grady*. Consequently, not only had I lost my manager to TV stardom, but I also had to make the long drive back to New York alone.

Now, eleven years later, with a sense of gloom surrounding our family excursion and with no pressing need to be there within a few days, we took a much more leisurely pace, making frequent stops to relax and enjoy the scenery. This tour of the vast American landscape proved to be one of our most enlightening and enjoyable family experiences. It was during this week-long westbound trek, however, that Sharon and I received word of my father's death, exactly three weeks after my fortieth birthday. We arrived in Los Angeles just two days before the funeral and burial services at Veterans Cemetery. Roscoe Irving Orman was just fifty-nine years old, and my bereavement, although far less anguished than that which had accompanied the deaths of Hunter and Nanny thirteen years earlier, was nonetheless genuine in its recognition of a life of lost promises, of gifts strewn upon a wasteland of misfortune, and of all the pain and sorrow of the lives left behind.

Another odd counterpoint to this mournful occasion, besides Sharon's being six months' pregnant with Miles, was the fact that Los Angeles was simultaneously hosting the 1984 Summer Olympics. The entire city contained an atmosphere of heightened celebration. We didn't attend any of the games, given the sad circumstances of our visit, but we did watch them on TV and couldn't help being affected by the sense of excitement that this spectacular global event had created throughout the entire city. In fact, the powerful symbolism inherent in the Olympic tradition, with its ceremonial passing of the torch, seemed to crystallize the themes of rebirth and renewal that were so germane to this moment.

Another major occurrence for me in 1984 was the filming of *Follow That Bird* in Toronto, Canada, during the month of August. A co-production of CTW and Warner Brothers, *Bird* was the first *Sesame Street* feature film and my first time working on the big screen since *Willie Dynamite*. I had auditioned, unsuccessfully, for virtually all of the scant roles available to black actors during this post-"blaxploitation" period, an era when the comic genius of Richard Pryor reigned supreme and which also preceded the career-making films of such future celluloid stars as Eddie Murphy, Whoopi Goldberg, Danny Glover, Morgan Freeman, Samuel L. Jackson, Denzel Washington, Alfre Woodard, Angela Bassett, Wesley Snipes, and Lawrence Fishburne or of such gifted black directors as Spike Lee, John Singleton, Bill Duke, and Carl Franklin. These and other artists would emerge during the mid to late eighties to usher in a new era of opportunity in Hollywood, at least for a select few. In the meantime, a key supporting role in a Warner Brothers family film, with a five-week summer shoot in lovely Toronto, was, for me, a welcome re-entry into movie making.

Two key members of the *Sesame Street* family, however, Jon Stone, the show's original producer/director and head writer who had hired most, if not all, of the existing cast, and Northern J. Calloway, who had been playing the part of David since the early seventies, were, to the dismay of many of us, inexplicably absent from this momentous endeavor. An up-and-coming young film director named Ken Kwapis was brought in from Hollywood by Warner Brothers to head the project. In spite of the intrigue surrounding these key decisions, the experience of working in the extremely hospitable city of Toronto, with its great restaurants, hotels, shops and nearby countryside, could hardly have been more enjoyable. The shoot resembled an extended holiday more than a five-week stint of tedious film-making. With our daughters vacationing with relatives in Mobile, Sharon joined me for the last few weeks of the shoot, and on our return home from Canada, we stopped in Buffalo, New York, to attend a performance of the spectacular Jackson Victory Concert that was touring the globe that year. What a thrill to have personally witnessed this early stage of the now legendary emergence of Michael Jackson as the premier performer of the 1980s! Even the unborn baby Miles, according to Sharon, couldn't resist moving to the pulsating beat of Michael, Jermaine, Tito, Jackie, Marlon, and Randy strutting their stuff under the starlit summer sky at Buffalo's Rice Stadium (home of the Bills). Just over three months later Miles Hunter Orman came into this world as a twenty-two-inch, ten-pound, one-and-three-quarter ounce bouncing bundle of joy.

Me and Sharon with "baby" Miles, December 4th, 1984.

With Lily Tomlin as Ernestine the operator. (Courtesy of Sesame Workshop.)

Loretta and me with Gladys Knight. (Courtesy of Sesame Workshop.)

Loretta, Bob, and I back up "Cousin" Ray Charles, 1992. (Courtesy of Sesame Workshop.)

SESAME STREET cast photo with Top L-R: Alison Bartlett (O'Reilly), Savion Glover, Elmo, Loretta Long, Miles Orman, me, Big Bird, Grundgetta the Grouch, Lilias White, David Langston Smyrl. Middle L-R: Linda Bove, Gladys the Cow, Bob McGrath, Bert, Ernie, Sonia Manzano, Emilio Delgado, Gabrielle Regan, Count Von Count, Oscar the Grouch, Roxie Marie, and Cookie Monster. Bottom L-R: Unknown child, Rosita, Unknown child, Baby Alice, Unknown child, Prairie Dawn, Telly Monster, Bill McCutcheon, and Baby Natasha, 1992. (Courtesy of Sesame Workshop.)

CHAPTER ELEVEN
New Vistas

FREEDOM

The sunlight seeps into my dreams like whiteout
As I shuffle-step awake toward morning
Doing the do that I do when I do
As the clock ticks in to the rhythm of my limbs
Painting the pattern of my day, my life, my self
Here in suburbia
But the need for change absorbs my brain
Taunting that half-sleeping inner-terrain
Where dreams still inhabit the invisible ditch
And the coffee kicks in to quicken the itch
Gotta move, gotta do, gotta find something new to need
Here in suburbia
Gotta find something new to feed
Both in word and in deed
That is relevant
That reaches deep and far and in-between the lies
Here in suburbia
That can feel the truth behind the eyes,
Beyond the skies,
And turn it into freedom.

11/4/98

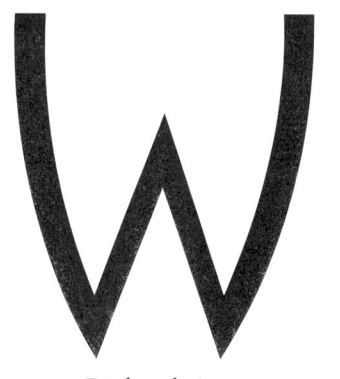ith a brand new baby boy and another feature film under my belt, I stepped into 1985 newly energized and optimistic about the future. In early spring my agent, Richard Astor, received a call from casting director Alex Gordon requesting to see me about a supporting role in a New York–based film from Orion Pictures, a crime caper starring Brian Dennehy and Bryan Brown, called *F/X*. Alex, who had cast me years earlier as police Lieutenant Connors opposite Telly Savalas in *Kojak*, knew that I could easily handle the assignment, but the movie's director, Robert Mandell, who at the time was the father of a four year-old daughter and a fan of *Sesame Street*, seemed genuinely surprised at my ability to play a hard-nosed New York police captain, a sharp contrast to the genial Gordon. Well written, acted, and directed, with a supporting cast that included Mason Adams, Jerry Orbach, Diane Venora, Cliff De Young, Trey Wilson, and Joe Grifasi, *F/X*, a production of Dodi Fayed (who a decade later would die tragically with his fiancée Princess Diana of England) became one of 1986's sleeper hits in theaters and even more popular later on video. In spite of its relative success, however, *F/X* would fail to significantly boost the careers of any of its participants, with the possible exception of Brian Dennehy, who was already on a roll with such films as *10, Silverado*, and *Cocoon*. My relatively small role as Dennehy's boss, Jake Wallinger, did little to enhance any bids of mine for film jobs in the following years. On the other hand, in addition to my *Gordon of Sesame Street* concerts having become more popular than ever, a new story line on *Sesame Street* would lead to one of the most uniquely fulfilling experiences of my life, and at the end of the '80s the New York theater world would provide me with two extraordinary high points.

Sometime in early 1985 during a *Sesame Street* taping session, Caroll Spinney and his wife Debra, in the course of admiring some recent

Publicity photo of Gordon, Susan, and baby Miles, 1985. (Courtesy of Sesame Workshop.)

photos of baby Miles with me, wondered aloud as to why Susan and Gordon, as the neighborhood's long-standing symbols of marital stability, should not also have a child. This simple question set into motion a chain of suggestions and discussions which led, eventually, to the introduction of 11-month-old Miles as the adopted son of Gordon and Susan Robinson of *Sesame Street*. In addition to giving honor and attention to the subject of adoption, the story line became the first on the show to involve the portrayal of a parent-child relationship among the regular cast (Buffy Sainte-Marie, who performed on the show for two seasons in the mid-'70s, made a few appearances with her son Cody prior to the introduction of Miles, and Gabrielle Regan, Sonia Manzano's daughter, would later play Gabby, the child of Maria and Luis). We even included a few visits by Susan's parents, Miles' grandparents (played beautifully by Frances Foster and Bill Cobbs). This development presented me with the most rewarding and challenging opportunity of my entire tenure on *Sesame Street*. Rasheda and Solana had each appeared on the show with me a few times, but not as my daughters. They, like all the other children, were kids in the neighborhood who had no familial bond with Gordon, or anyone else on the show. By contrast, the addition of Miles

Family portrait with Solana, me, Miles, Sharon, and Rasheda, 1985.

created a completely new dynamic within the program. As both my real and my fictitious son, his presence immediately raised the stakes of my commitment, as well as that of the producers, to the principles of parenting and role-modeling. More importantly for me, it provided a unique bonding experience for Miles and me during his most formative years, which has greatly enhanced and continues to inform our relationship.

Early in 1987, documentary filmmaker and longtime friend St. Clair Bourne invited me to participate in a film of his about the life and work of the great twentieth-century poet Langston Hughes. Entitled *Langston Hughes: The Dream Keeper*, the production was part of PBS's *Voices and Visions* series to be shown nationwide various times during the following year. St. Clair used several performers, including Novella Nelson, Diane McIntyre, Olu Dara, Max Roach, David Langston Smyrl, Bob Macbeth, and me, to help dramatize several of Hughes' more visually interpretive works. In addition, he used the voices of Novella and me reciting the poems and prose of Langston to serve as the narrative voice for the entire film. This was not only a sound creative idea beautifully realized but, personally, it also afforded me my first opportunity to enter the world of documentary film narration, a field which I had been aspiring to pursue for some time. I thoroughly enjoyed the experience of employing my voice in this way, especially in a context as compelling as the life and works of one the century's most revered poets (whose inclusion of me in his book *Black Magic* some 25 years earlier had so highlighted the beginning of my career). Furthermore, St. Clair, whose work I had long admired and with whom I had been friends since the early days of New Lafayette, is an artist whose personal temperament and esthetic sensibility are as close to my own as any I've encountered. This feeling of compatibility has resulted in several other assignments by him to narrate his films. Over the years, our relationship has continued to grow into what I consider to be among my most treasured and enduring alliances.

By late 1987 it had been over three and a half years since *Twenty Year Friends*, the longest I had ever gone without doing a play since my career had started in '62. So when Lloyd Richards offered me the job of replacing Frankie Faison on Broadway as Gabriel in August Wilson's Tony

Award– and Pulitzer Prize–winning play *Fences*, I was chomping at the bit and ready to devour this wonderful role. The play, with its record-breaking run, had become a milestone in theater history, not to mention in the careers of all of its principal players. Wilson and Richards had scored a more modest success a few years earlier in the fall of 1984 with their collaboration on *Ma Rainey's Black Bottom*, which introduced the forceful Charles S. Dutton to New York theater audiences. *Ma Rainey* had also helped to revive the careers of stage veterans Theresa Merritt, Joe Seneca, Leonard Jackson, and Robert Judd. *Fences*, however, became the most critically and commercially successful play by an African-American to appear on Broadway since Lloyd's legendary staging of Lorraine Hansbury's *A Raisin in the Sun* in 1959. Cutting across social and racial lines with its universal family themes, this sensational drama, set in 1950s Pittsburgh (Wilson's native city), garnered nearly every major award in several categories, including Lead Actor for James Earl Jones in a towering performance as the fictitious ex–Negro League baseball slugger Troy Maxon, his best role since Jack Jefferson in *The Great White Hope* some twenty years earlier. *Fences* re-established him as one of America's most formidable theater talents. Well-deserved recognition also went to newcomer Courtney B. Vance as Troy's son Cory and to my dear friend Mary Alice for yet another breath-taking display of acting prowess as Rose, Troy's steadfast and long-suffering wife. For his performance as Gabriel, Frankie had also received a Tony nomination as Best Featured Actor.

Most of the play's roles were being recast simultaneously, with Billy Dee Williams replacing James Earl as Troy, Lynne Thigpen coming in for Mary, Vince Williams for Charles Brown as Troy's older son Lyons, Courtney's understudy Byron Mimms replacing him as Cory, and me, with only Ray Aranha and young Tatyana Ali staying on from the original cast.

My inheritance of this wonderfully colorful, hauntingly idiosyncratic role was truly a Godsend. I had never before played a character quite like Gabriel. Troy's younger brother by seven years and a World War II veteran, Gabe, as everyone called him, carried around a beat-up bugle on a string. A metal plate inside his head as a remnant of surgery for a war injury had diminished much of his mental capacity but, conversely, seemed to enhance his powers of empathy and spiritual "vision." The key to this childlike, but deceptively serious character was in his utter goodness and his strong connection to a higher power. Believing himself to be Gabriel the Archangel, whose mission it was to open the gates of heaven to his brother Troy, Gabe supplied the play with both levity and enormous depth, a rare and sublime combination. I relished every performance of this intriguing, exhilarating role for our six-month run (the longest I'd ever experienced) at Broadway's splendid 46th Street Theatre before mostly capacity audiences. Even though as replacements we were not eligible for awards and received only a few scant notices, *Variety* Magazine called my interpretation of Gabe a "gem."

Me as Gabriel in the Broadway production of FENCES, 1988.

This six-month period during which we completed the record-setting year-and-a-half run of *Fences* (March '87 through June '88) was a time of unprecedented abundance for black theater artists on Broadway. *Sarafina*, Mbongeni Ngema's high-spirited South African musical import depicting the student uprisings of Soweto, was enjoying a long and successful run at Broadway's Cort Theatre. *Gospel at Colonus*, Lee Breuer's musical based on the Oedipus legend starring Morgan Freeman, Carl Lumbly, and a host of Gospel greats that included the Five Blind Boys of Alabama, was transplanted from the Brooklyn Academy of Music to Broadway's Lunt-Fontanne for a short run. *Oba Oba*, a musical spectacle from Brazil, was running at the Ambassador Theatre. And, finally, August Wilson's third play to reach Broadway under Lloyd Richards' direction, *Joe Turner's Come and Gone*, a richly textured, compelling family drama also set in Wilson's Pittsburgh, but in the early 1900s, had opened that March at Broadway's Barrymore to reviews comparable to those for *Fences*. With standout performances by Delroy Lindo, Angela Bassett, L. Scott Caldwell, Mel Winkler, and others, *Joe*

Turner put August and Lloyd in the unprecedented position of having two successful Broadway productions running simultaneously. During the spring of '88 Richard Gant, Karen Allen Baxter, and Duma Ndlovu organized a gathering of theater artists at Lincoln Center to celebrate the historical nature of this moment, hoping to provide a much needed shot of encouragement in the arm of black theater. This event served as both a reunion of sorts for the many theater veterans who attended and also as an opportunity to applaud, support, and validate all who had survived and were participating in the current prosperity. The phenomenal success of the Wilson/Richards team especially seemed to signal within the ranks of our colleagues and supporters, at least in spirit, a kind of renaissance; or perhaps we all just felt the need to acknowledge and savor this rare moment in time. In any event, by year's end all of the above plays had closed and, since then, the fortunes of black theater (certainly on Broadway) have never even come close to duplicating such bounty.

My own continuing good fortune during 1988, however, was enhanced by two unusually interesting television assignments that year. While still doing *Fences* I was offered one of the two starring roles in a TV pilot project entitled *Hard Time on Planet Earth,* for which I took a week's leave-of-absence from the play to fly to Los Angeles and perform. A co-production of CBS Television and Disney Studios, *Hard Time* was a sci-fi story revolving around an alien creature, played by Martin Kove, who is banished to earth to do penance for some infraction on his native planet. Producer-director Robert Mandell, who had directed me in *F/X*, cast me once again as a police officer, Captain Rawlings, who pursues the elusive extra-terrestrial as he precariously acquaints himself with life on earth. The script, written by the highly respected team of the Thomas brothers, Jim and John (*Predator*), had real promise but, due to a writer's strike in effect at the time, was ineligible for re-writes during production. This severely limited us to the less-than-ready versions. Consequently, the pilot, which was to be run in early 1989, lacked sufficient strength to be considered for a regular slot on CBS.

The second TV assignment I was offered came in the fall of that year from another friend and former associate Stan Lathan, who had, some fifteen years earlier, suggested that I audition for *Sesame Street*. Stan hired me to do a guest spot on the ABC series *A Man Called Hawk*, a spin-off in which Avery Brooks reprised the role that he had originated on the highly successful *Spencer for Hire* with Robert Urich. Filmed in Washington, D.C., *Hawk* revolved around the exploits of Avery's unorthodox private-eye character, an ex-prizefighter, bodyguard, and connoisseur of the arts. I had only one scene as Malcolm, a Muslim prison inmate and old friend of Hawk's from whom he solicits some crucial information and insight. Brief though it was, I enjoyed this chance to reunite with my old colleagues Stan and Avery.

With Akosua Bosia in THE TALENTED TENTH, Manhattan Theatre Club, 1989.

To my surprise and delight, the last year of the 1980s began with another long overdue reunion when I was offered the lead role in the Manhattan Theatre Club's premiere production of old friend Richard Wesley's ambitious and challenging political romance, *The Talented Tenth*. Set in the late 1980s, this timely drama depicted the events revolving around the mid-life crisis of '60s college radical and civil rights activist turned '80s corporate success, Bernard Evans, a top-dog programming executive at a black-owned radio station. Supremely gifted, motivated, and accomplished, Bernard has reached a point in life when all that he has worked to achieve over the last twenty years suddenly strikes him as devoid of meaning and far from what he had originally set out to accomplish. This catapults him into a frenzy of self-destructive behavior, resulting in the eventual loss of his marriage, family, and career. In the course of his downfall, however, Bernard seems to rediscover a spiritual core and a clarity that has long been missing in his life and which, presumably, will help him in the pursuit of a new and more meaningful path.

This play, with its complex themes of political and moral integrity, economic independence, marital infidelity, and spiritual redemption proved to be one of the most provocative and intriguing among Wesley's long list of compelling social dramas. And the role of Bernard was easily among the most challenging and complicated I'd encountered in some time. The Harlem-bred and West Coast–based TV and film director M. Neema Barnette staged the production. It had a cinematic fluidity which was utterly captivating and boasted a carefully selected all-star cast of players that included Sonny Jim Gaines, Richard Gant, Marie Thomas, Akosua Bosia, LaTanya Richardson, Rony Clanton, and Elain Graham. Relegated by MTC to its smaller experimental stage rather than the main stage at its new City Center home, this intellectually and emotionally stimulating production, although neither advertised nor reviewed by the media, became, through word of mouth alone, one of the hottest tickets of the season. Towards the end of its extended five-week run it was enthusiastically attended (in several cases more than once) by many within the artistic and political communities, including such luminaries as Ossie Davis and Ruby Dee, Stevie Wonder, Melba Moore, Susan B. Taylor, and the Reverend Calvin O. Butts, to name a few.

As had been the case with most of my theatrical assignments since the late seventies, the commitment to do *The Talented Tenth* involved a limitation on the number of personal appearance engagements I could assume during the run and/or the producer's agreement to allow me to miss a few performances in order to do a date or two. In this case, the missed performances came near the end of the run and required that my understudy, James Pickens Jr., replace me for one weekend. Such an arrangement, inconvenient though it may have been, was a financial necessity on my part, with a "Gordon" date paying roughly ten times my weekly salary for the play. So my missing a few shows was something I could easily accept. What followed in the weeks and months immediately after the run of *Tenth*, however, was not as easy to swallow.

Unlike the scenario of twelve years earlier following the run of *The Last Street Play*, all attempts by Richard and Lynne Meadow to move *The Talented Tenth* beyond its showcase status up to that of a more commercial platform were met by failure. Despite the superior quality of all of its components, the apparent stumbling block was in the serious nature of its subject matter. A powerfully relevant black political drama seemed to be more than the "mainstream" theater establishment could handle, dooming it to remain marginally categorized, something which we all found extremely disappointing but not at all surprising. It seemed, in fact, that most of our theatrical careers had followed this pattern. With *The Last Street Play*, the work had been misguidedly re-fashioned to make it more palatable to a Broadway audience. Fortunately, in the case of *Talented Tenth*, no such attempt was made. So when the five-week run came to a close, we all, as had become the custom, folded our tent, each moving on to his or her next assignment. In parting, I made it abundantly clear to Richard and Lynne that the chances of my being available to them at a later date, should the play be revived, would be exceedingly slim.

Sure enough, a few months later, just as I was about to begin my fifteenth season on *Sesame Street*, I received a call from Richard, asking that I meet him for lunch at Manhattan Plaza later that week to discuss plans to revive the show, this time on the main stage at MTC. I went to the meeting knowing that I would be unable to bring myself to such a commitment unless, somehow, the production would accommodate itself to my upcoming taping and personal appearance schedules. As expected, Richard and Lynne could not agree to such an accommodation and I had to confront the painful irony of the situation staring me in the face.

Twelve years earlier I had been denied an opportunity, by the same parties mind you, to advance an important role (and possibly my career) to another level, and now here I was about to turn down a proposition to do the very same thing. Intensifying the problem was the fact that, at the age of forty-five, there was presumably more at stake than there had been at age thirty-three. How many more such chances would come my way? The worst part of this predicament, however, even more than any feelings of professional loss, was the guilt that I felt for having to abandon my fellow players, denying them and the production of my contribution to the delicately constructed ensemble that we had all worked so hard to create.

Adding to my anguish, Richard Gant, the only cast member who had also been a part of the *Last Street Play/Mighty Gents* fiasco, came to pay me a surprise visit during a *Sesame Street* taping session with a final plea that I reconsider and agree to do the play. I did feel somewhat less tortured in making my final determination, however, by the fact that, weeks earlier, Sonny Jim Gaines had, inexplicably and to the chagrin of myself and other cast members, been dropped and replaced with Graham Brown, a decision which I considered both ethically and artistically misguided as well as a personal affront. Sonny Jim had given a typically solid performance as Mr. Griggs, the mentor and father figure to Bernard, a relationship similar to that which we had shared ten years earlier as Caesar and Brutus. Our work together in both these productions had been informed by twenty years of friendship, collaboration, and trust. Although these sentiments bore no reflection upon Graham, with whom I had worked in *The Great MacDaddy* and both liked and respected, frankly, this move by Lynne, Neema, and especially Richard, who had borne personal witness to the long alliance between Sonny and myself, did affect me and the intensity of my commitment to the production.

Richard Lawson, a West Coast actor whom I had first met as a rival for the role of Willie Dynamite in 1973 and whom I had later seen perform the part of Frankie Sojourner in Joe Papp's Mobile Unit production of *The Mighty Gents* (which also featured Bill Cobbs, Gary Bolling, and a young Denzel Washington) was chosen to succeed me in the role of Bernard. A likable and attractive actor, Lawson, in my estimation, had neither the technical skill, the presence, nor the emotional range required to successfully pull off this complex role. I received no comfort in that fact, and, indeed, when critics roundly attacked his performance, and subsequently the play, it truly pained me to read the reviews. I felt especially bad for the remaining original cast members, all of whom deserved much better. Of course, and in spite of myself, I couldn't help but wonder "what if...."

Even if not a commercial hit, an extended, upscale, and critically successful run of *The Talented Tenth* would have at least served notice that there were still black theater artists able and willing to confront some of the more serious contemporary issues stemming from the legacy of the previous two decades.

SESAME STREET cast with Patti LaBelle in Roaring Twenties scene. Emilio, Loretta, Patti LaBelle, me, Sonia, and Bob. (Courtesy of Sesame Workshop.)

With jazzman James Moody. (Photo by Alicia Tilque.)

With blues great B.B. King. (Photo by Gordon Price.)

With Gregory Hines.

With Cheech Marin.

CHAPTER TWELVE
Toward the Light

ANGELIC PRAYER

In the blind night or the glare of day
when the mash and madness strikes
and strands us in the wild
We pray
to bring forth
in the cool wakeful light
of here and now,
the present mind,
forever in the moment,
with the full-winged, tender vision
of the holy soldiers.
And as our better selves emerge
Awake and True and Whole,
We drink it in, exhale,
and give thanks for this angelic glow
which permeates the density
of life.

12/19/99

The disappointments arising out of my theater experiences in the late 1980s had been like déjà vu. The level of professional recognition and respect which seemed to have repeatedly come within my reach had once again eluded me. Consequently, I entered the nineties even more wary than usual of subjecting myself again to the vagaries and variances of an industry which was obviously influenced far more by economic greed than by artistic merit, particularly when it came to artists of color. And so, relying once again upon the safety net of *Sesame Street*, I vigorously pursued those endeavors which had provided me with nearly two decades of a measure of prestige and security. Although not at all immune to the same forces that had come to redefine the entertainment industry in general, my *Sesame Street* colleagues and I, as recognizable icons of CTW's flagship production, still enjoyed an enviable combination of stability, availability, and creative and moral sustenance. And as *Sesame Street* began to approach its twenty-fifth and then its thirtieth year of production, the level of celebration and recognition for the show's remarkable success and its enormous contribution to the world's children would become amplified to a degree unprecedented, not only in our history, but in that of the entire industry.

The phenomenal longevity of *Sesame Street* and its resulting preeminence had, paradoxically, also helped to intensify the perennial dilemma of trying to build a legitimate acting career from an increasingly entrenched status as a children's public television icon. Back in 1977, during the rehearsal period for *The Last Street Play*, I vividly remember Morgan Freeman expressing his relief concerning the cancellation the previous year of *The Electric Company*, CTW's sister series to *Sesame Street*. "Roscoe," he said, "this has been a blessing in disguise." Morgan had played the character Easy Reader for the entire five-year run of the show. Although he had had initial feelings of concern about the sudden loss of income resulting from this termination, he said that he had also found great comfort in the knowledge that he would not be forever associated with this one character from a children's TV show. I completely understood this sentiment. The fact is that for a good number of our viewers we have come to be seen not as actors or even entertainers but as endearing and familiar personalities who happen to be on TV. Some, upon meeting us, are surprised and disappointed to discover that most of us do not actually bear the same names as our TV characters. This kind of misunderstanding of who and what we are has, for seasoned theater veterans like Emilio Delgado (Luis), Linda Bove (Linda), Sonia Manzano (Maria), Alison Bartlett (Gina), and me, compounded the task of distinguishing ourselves as members of the larger community of working professional actors. None of us, for example, has ever been even *nominated* for the coveted Daytime Emmy Award, a trophy which, ironically, *Sesame Street* itself has *won* more times than *any* other program in the history of television.

Generally speaking, the adult human characters on the show, as compared to our Muppet colleagues, have traditionally held a tenuous and somewhat less secure position within the framework of the company's corporate vision. This relationship was strongly underlined in the course of a collective bargaining dispute between CTW and the entire group of performers sometime during the late 1970s. Faced with the prospect of having to pay us what we thought we were worth to the show, the Workshop (under the leadership of its then executive

Dressed to kill at the Emmy Awards: Bob McGrath, me, Sonia Manzano, Caroll Spinney, Brian Muehl, Alaina Reed, Emilio Delgado, Rob Gardner, Will Lee, Loretta Long, and Jerry Nelson, 1982.

producer Al Hyslop) abruptly resorted to "hard-ball" tactics. Late one evening I received a phone call from close friend Maurice Woods who immediately inquired as to whether or not I had recently been offered a major Hollywood contract. "No," I replied, "Why do you ask?" To which he answered "Well, tomorrow I have an appointment to audition for the role of 'Gordon' on *Sesame Street*." Suddenly confronted with the possibility of becoming unemployed, within a few days the spirit of our coalition had been broken, forcing us each to scramble individually to save our jobs and settle for whatever deal we were offered.

Within the industry-at-large, unlike many of our fellow actors in prime-time commercial television, we are seldom considered for roles that would either enhance our stature or allow potential employers to use our tenured visibility as a possible advantage for a given project. Instead, we are viewed by many as celebrated and admirable but "not-ready-for-prime-time" supporting players, with the prevailing wisdom being (at least among the powers that be) that we are less viable as marketable performers than those whose names and faces have been directly associated with the selling of theater tickets or commercial products (such as our Muppet counterparts). This distinction is especially frustrating in light of the fact that in recent years an increasing number of entertainers have begun to move freely between the worlds of television, movies, concerts, live theater, and nightclubs with little or no stigma derived from this mobility. Unfortunately, this narrow perception of us is sometimes accompanied by a lack of respect, although usually from people whose attitudes are clearly based upon ignorance and/or envy.

On a deeper level, however, these types of divisions and classifications within the entertainment industry are by-products of the age-old Hollywood star system, a hierarchy whose economics are based upon a set of criteria which, although maddeningly elusive, are often calculatedly superficial, sexist, racist, homophobic, and elitist. The early architects of Hollywood who became the dream-makers of twentieth-century American popular culture were, in the name of profit, more than willing to often use their formidable machinery to perpetuate and glorify the most perverse and destructive impulses within our society (e.g., D.W. Griffith's *Birth of a Nation*). Certainly by omission and by the blatant use of vicious stereotypes but mostly through the mass creation and distribution of a seemingly "benign" imagery, our entertainment industry has systematically and unquestioningly fostered, among other myths, the concept of white superiority and hegemony. Consequently, an all-out war against the status-quo mentality supporting this insidious set of presumptions has historically been the birthright of every person marginalized by color, ethnicity, or social conscience to have worked within the conjoining fields of art, entertainment, and commerce. Hence, we have the towering legacies of such nineteenth- and twentieth-century titans as Ira Aldridge, W.E.B. DuBois, Paul Robeson, Oscar Micheaux, Zora Neale Hurston, Josephine Baker, Langston Hughes, Richard Wright, James Baldwin, and countless others whose lives and careers were characterized by endless struggle in the face of an intransigent and reactionary American popular culture. I entered the 1990s with an acute personal awareness of this history and more resolve than ever to somehow absorb and reflect the legacy of this struggle and to add my voice, in some meaningful way, to the long chorus of testifiers to this truth. Little would I have guessed the specific course this mission would take.

By 1990 it had been five years with no follow-up film work since *F/X*. Given my relatively high hopes immediately after its release of at least securing an occasional movie supporting role, especially with the advent of Spike Lee's prominence and of star-making turns by such stalwarts as friends Morgan Freeman and Sam Jackson, I began to lose patience with the seeming inability of Richard Astor, my agent since 1976, to take better advantage of my past experiences and move my career along in a way more in line with these goals. I expressed my concerns to Richard and also to several friends who I felt could lend a sympathetic ear. One such person was Broadway veteran Lilias White, who had added her warm and engaging persona and enormous gifts as a singer and actress to the regular cast of *Sesame Street* the previous year as Lillian the daycare worker. Visiting the set one day with her daughter, Lilias's agent Meg Mortimer approached me (in much the same way as Richard had done some fifteen years earlier) offering me her card with an invitation to call and discuss the possibility of her representing me. It seemed as though fate were answering my call. I could sense in Meg the kind of drive and proficiency that I felt was, by then, so lacking in Richard. In my first meeting with her I also came to discover that she was in partnership with Lou Ambrosio, who had started the agency a few years earlier and, after setting up Meg in their fully staffed New York office, migrated to Hollywood to establish the West Coast arm of the growing Ambrosio/Mortimer Agency. I further learned that she and Lou had helped guide the careers of such up-and-coming talents as Sam Jackson, Angela Bassett, and Charles S. Dutton, to name a few. Needless to say, I was impressed. It didn't take much effort on Meg's part to convince me that she and Lou could provide much better representation, on both coasts, than Richard, with his minuscule office and meager two-man staff, could possibly do.

In spite of all these glaring advantages, however, the act of ending my fifteen years of representation by the Richard Astor Agency was one of the single most excruciating decisions of my professional life. I agonized for weeks over just how I would break the news to Richard who, after all, was guilty of nothing more than being less than fully equipped to provide what I thought necessary for the advancement of my career at this time. To my knowledge, he had never deceived me nor been less than fully committed to my continued employment within this insanely competitive industry. I had, over the years, heard reports of his being somewhat abrasive in his dealings with prospective employers but considered that trait as a possible advantage for an agent in the dog-eat-dog world of show business.

Furthermore, throughout this period Richard was more familiar than anyone with the qualitative scope and depth of my work in both theater and film, becoming, in the process, a reliable barometer for my own assessment of the incremental growth and variation along my artistic path. This particular aspect of our relationship, so subtle in nature, was, unfortunately, taken far too much for granted by me, and it was only in hindsight that I began to appreciate the value which it brought to my craft. For this and other reasons which I could not have predicted, I would eventually come to regret, or at least second-guess, my decision to leave Richard.

Over the next three or four years the efforts of Meg Mortimer's New York team began to bear some fruit. After securing a few small supporting roles in two East Coast–based feature films (Rowdy Herrington's *Striking Distance* starring Bruce Willis, in which I played a homicide detective, and Nick Gomez's *New Jersey Drive*, in which I played a judge for the first time) and a number of unsuccessful attempts at booking my first network television pilot since the ill-fated *Hard Time on Planet Earth*, I was offered a central supporting role on an ABC-TV situation comedy prospect based on the stand-up material of a West Coast comic by the name of Jack Gallagher. Entitled *Bringing Up Jack*, the show revolved around the work and family life of Jack's character, a sports talk-show host at a San Francisco radio station of which my character was the owner. In its similarity to Edward Asner's Lou Grant character of *Mary Tyler Moore Show* fame, I thought that my role had the potential, if the show were successful, of making me a recognizable fixture in prime-time TV land. In the course of rehearsal and taping in Los Angeles, however, it soon became apparent to me that my character, the only one of the regulars cast with a non-white actor, was little more than a token figure in a portrait of lily-white Americana. Consequently, despite the inclusion of the talented Harley Jane Kozak in the role of Jack's wife, Jeff Garlin as Jack's sidekick, and of L. Scott Caldwell in a small guest cameo as the family obstetrician, in addition to the spirited direction of former teen star Robbie Benson, my enthusiasm for the role and for the entire project quickly faded. My goal then became to collect the sizable salary for the few weeks of work with the hope that the program might quietly and unceremoniously disappear, as is the fate of the large majority of television pilots. And, after nearly a year of "wait and see," that is exactly what happened.

Meanwhile, back in the late summer of 1991 I had received a call from Bill Lathan informing me of a one-man play entitled *Folks Remembers: The Rise and Fall of Harlem*, which our friend Sonny Jim Gaines had written for himself and would be performing the following week at what used to be the old Equity Library Theatre, now called the Majestic, on West 103rd Street near Riverside Drive. Aided by Andre Mtumi's direction, Sonny offered a tour-de-force portrayal of Folks, a man who, like himself, had lived for many years in Harlem and witnessed several of its major transformations, accumulating along the way a wealth of knowledge and wisdom, despite the fact that he was presently unemployed and homeless. The play was in two acts and during the intermission I receded to the lobby to "chew the fat" with several old friends, including Andre, Billy, George Miles, and to my surprise, Matt Robinson, whom I hadn't seen in quite some time. In recent years Matt had moved on from *Sesame Street* to other ventures, eventually becoming a writer and producer on the landmark *Cosby Show* of the 1980s. In the course of our conversation, he mentioned that he had a script which he wanted me to read, not specifying either its title or its subject. A few days later I received a package containing Matt's manuscript. I was startled and intrigued by the provocative title, *The Confessions of Stepin Fetchit*.

For several years, long before witnessing Sonny Jim's *Folks*, I had begun to entertain the idea of performing a one-character piece. Undoubtedly, I was attracted by the challenge of carrying an evening of theater all alone, as tempting a test and a showcase of one's acting skills as I could imagine. I vividly remember my first time seeing an actor single-handedly hold an audience's attention for a full evening when, in 1965, Ruby Dee performed various characters in a one-woman show at the Baton Rouge, Louisiana, campus of Southern University. Several of us from FST had driven the two hours from New Orleans for the experience of observing this consummate artist as she wielded her craft to mesmerize all in attendance.

More recently, I had been both moved and enthralled by the one-person performances of John

Me with Telly, Ossie Davis, Ruby Dee, and Elmo. (Courtesy of Sesame Workshop.)

Leguizamo in his semi-autobiographical *Mambo Mouth*, of James Earl Jones as Paul Robeson in the Broadway production of Philip Hayes Dean's mono-drama *Robeson*, of Liz Van Dyke as writer Zora Neale Hurston in Lawrence Holder's *Zora*, and of Charles S. Dutton as the 19th-century Shakespearean actor Ira Aldridge in *Excellent Mummer*. Each of these performances aroused in me a combination of admiration, envy, and a desire to emulate their example by finding the appropriate vehicle for me to display my own skill and artistry within this milieu. I also relished the idea of once again portraying a real person for the first time since I had played Ike Hockenhull in *Mahalia*. All of the subjects which occurred to me, however, were rather obvious and safe examples of black historical achievers, such as George Washington Carver, General Benjamin O. Davis, and other acceptable icons of African-Americana. In light of this, the very notion of portraying a figure as politically "incorrect" and controversial as the infamous Stepin Fetchit shot a tantalizing bolt of fear through my heart, which would serve as a dare and a challenge to my pride as an artist of integrity and skill.

As it turns out, Billy had, more or less, orchestrated the coming together of Matt (whom he had also invited to Sonny's show) and me, with the intention of uniting the three of us in an effort to get *Confessions* produced. Billy wanted to direct and, possibly, produce the play as well, if no one else could be found. Matt had written the piece a decade earlier. It was based on conversations he'd had with the late Lincoln Perry, the actor who had created and become best known as the hilariously lazy Stepin Fetchit character of Hollywood's early talking films of the late 1920s through the early 1940s. In 1974, during the filming of *Amazing Grace*, a feature he had written and produced (with direction by Stan Lathan) as a vehicle for the legendary comedienne Jackie "Moms" Mabley, Matt was introduced one day by co-star Slappy White to Perry, who had come by to visit the set. Instantly smitten by Perry's gracious but powerful persona, as well as by his intriguing legacy, Matt offered him a small cameo in the film, initiating a friendship which lasted until Perry's death in 1985.

Matt's play is, essentially, Perry's own story in his own words, a remarkable tale of resourcefulness, talent, and amazing ambition in the face of nearly impossible odds, with phenomenal success followed by years of contempt and ridicule. I, like many blacks and others of my generation, grew up with scant knowledge of the Stepin Fetchit character known to millions of fans during the 1930s. By the time I was born in 1944, he and most of his fellow black performers of early Hollywood had become pariahs to the new upwardly mobile "pre–civil rights" generation. People like Perry, Hattie McDaniel, Mantan Moreland, Willie Best, Butterfly McQueen, Bill "Bojangles" Robinson and others who had opened the door for the next era of black artist/entertainers to walk through, were suddenly discarded in disgrace after a decade or more of adoration and immense prosperity. Even the great Louis Armstrong, who became a fixture in Hollywood films during that period, would surely have suffered a similar fate, had it not been for his musical genius, which appealed to almost all of America. Reading Matt's script, I was deeply touched by the beauty, humor, and pain of Perry's story, which resonated with layers of meaning around and within the history of blacks in America. The transcendent talents of artists like Perry and others were greatly exploited by the captains of the entertainment industry during the first half of the twentieth century only to be discarded and denigrated by them in subsequent years.

One of the most enlightening aspects of Lincoln Perry's story, and of Robinson's play, is the combination of ambition, guile, and gleeful duplicity with which he created and performed the comic Stepin Fetchit character, the subversive nature of which was shared with much of his black audience. Perry's humor was, in fact, rooted in a tradition which dated back to slavery times, one in which to feign dimwittedness or laziness was an act of defiance. As Perry says in the play:

> "The slaves, they used to love watchin' the lazy, shufflin', clownin' coons cause they knew there wasn't no reward for hard work, except more work. But if you could lazy your way outa some work, then you was beatin' slavery. The only reason they captured you in the first place was so you could work for free, and now you done found a way to beat them back."

White audiences on the other hand, by and large oblivious to this feature of the Fetchit persona, were equally captivated by Perry's hilarious antics and performing virtuosity. Throughout my research for the role, mostly in viewing hard-to-find archival footage of his early films, I was deeply impressed by Perry's uncanny natural screen presence and formidable gifts as a physical comic performer but even more so by his highly stylized, fearlessly brazen send-up of the hard-core racial stereotypes of his era. His career ascendancy occurred, one must remember, at a time when the routine lynching of black men was commonplace, when Jim Crow and segregation were acceptable practices to the majority of white America, and when the notion of a black man occupying a position of stature within the kingdom of Hollywood, even as the presumable "court jester," had to be considered a sign of "progress."

Between the time that I first received Matt's script and the eventual premiere of the play in early 1993, I was to also discover a surprising, almost eerie personal connection between myself and Lincoln Perry. In February of 1992, anxious to test the benefits of my newly acquired West Coast representation by Lou Ambrosio, I flew to L.A. shortly after the taping season for *Sesame Street* had ended, with hopes of possibly snaring some work on a film or a television pilot. My month-long visit, although unsuccessful in this regard, enabled me to also spend time with old friends Whitman and Gail Mayo, with whom I stayed, and Tommy Hicks, who had migrated and taken up residence there a few years earlier. I also got to visit my Aunt Cora several times, usually at her home, where we would sit and reminisce about family history, as had become our custom over the years. I was especially glad to see her around this time to share her joy in the recent and well-deserved recognition she was getting for her star performance in Julie Dash's breathtakingly beautiful independent film, *Daughters of the Dust*.

One evening, as Cora Lee relayed some tale involving her and my father as youngsters in Florida, she made a few references to someone named "Step" in connection to their mother, my grandmother, Rafaela Orman. By her third or fourth mention of this person, she added the surname "Fetchit" and my heartbeat quickened. How could this be? I had not, as yet, even mentioned Matt's play or the name Stepin Fetchit to Cora. To my recollection, this was the first time she had ever brought up his name to me. I began to bombard her with questions about her knowledge of Lincoln Perry and his connection to our family. As it turns out, Grandma and Perry, both natives of Key West, Florida, were born in the same year (1902) and, living across the street from each other throughout their childhood, developed a friendship that lasted for most of their lives. My father and Cora, as youngsters during the 1920s and 30s, knew "Step," not as a Hollywood actor, but as a family friend who would occasionally visit them and their mother at home. Aunt Cora even expressed some uncertainty about the extent of this relationship but had no hard evidence of anything more than a close friendship between her mother and "Uncle" Step.

Many years later, long after Grandma Rafaela's death in 1961, Cora, as an adult, became reunited with Perry during his years of convalescence at an actors' home in Los Angeles. A friendship evolved between them which lasted for the remainder of his life. She would call on him and exchange a flow of correspondence, all of which Cora eagerly shared with me. She was absolutely delighted to hear of my involvement with a play about Perry's career, having long felt that the life and reputation of her friend had been unduly slandered by fans and historians alike. Vividly relaying the astonishing contrast between the Stepin Fetchit screen persona known to moviegoers and the proud and charismatic personality of the actor who played him, Cora strongly pleaded that I make the effort to convey the sense of dignity and intelligence embodied by the Lincoln Perry that she knew and loved.

The impact of this revelation and the unbelievable convergence of circumstance surrounding it left me speechless. For as long as I can remember I've always believed in the power of divine guidance in my life, but my faith in God, stemming from those early years of instruction in the Catholic school tradition (which had also served as Lincoln Perry's educational foundation), had evolved through various forms and stages of intensity. Now, it seemed as though God had a clear and specific professional assignment designed just for me; that I use my craft to shed light upon the legacy of this misunderstood and much maligned man whose ambition, talent, tenacity, and pioneering spirit had helped to pave the way for the generations of black performers who would follow.

By February of 1993, after a year and a half of Matt and Billy's efforts to find a suitable theater and/or producer for *Confessions*, Wynn Handman began to express an interest in the play as a "limited run" offering in the smaller stage of the American Place Theatre. Over the years, I had come to know and respect Handman as both an acting teacher of great renown, with such former students as Dustin Hoffman and Denzel Washington, and also as a producer of uncommon courage and vision. Beginning with the three Bullins plays in '68, when his theater was located at St. Clement's Church on West 46th Street, and his subsequent productions of such gems as *La Tourista* by Sam Shepard, Charlie Russell's *Five on the Black Hand Side*, Ed Bullins' *Pig Pen*, Philip Hayes Dean's *Every Night When the Sun Goes Down*, James De Jongh's *Do Lord Remember Me*, John Leguizamo's *Mambo Mouth*, and many more, Wynn has, over the course of time, proven himself to be a man of uncompromising artistic integrity whose choices have, unlike those of many of his counterparts, always been based upon the intrinsic quality and power of the material rather than its commercial appeal.

There were, however, two conditions that came with his agreement to do the play. First, in light of the controversial nature of our piece, and as a way of reviving an old tradition of his theater, Wynn asked that we include a post-play discussion after each performance. Second, due both to financial constraints and his seasonal calendar, which required that a production be slotted for the following month, Wynn wanted us to begin rehearsals immediately so that performances could commence in three weeks.

To his first request, I was more or less agreeable, having favorably experienced a similar tradition during my Free Southern Theater days. Billy was less enthusiastic, feeling that, in general, post-play discussions were anti-climactic appendages of works that should speak for themselves. As a general principle I agreed with him, but I could also see how an audience's open discussion of this particular play and the issues inherent to it could be an extremely dynamic addendum with a life of its own. As to Wynn's second request, we both felt that, in spite of the extra pressure of having so little time to prepare, we were up to the task. Although we hadn't worked together since *The Sirens* nearly twenty years earlier, Billy and I had, after all, been part of one of the most accomplished ensembles in theater history. During our New Lafayette days, in fact, we did play after play, usually rehearsing four weeks or less, and yet, due to the highly evolved rapport within our ranks, repeatedly achieved wondrous results. Furthermore, the specific chemistry between Billy and me, having evolved over some twenty-five years, had coalesced into a uniquely intuitive combination of mutual respect and affection, allowing for an effective method of shorthand communication in our rehearsals. Based upon an implicit friendship and trust, this method gave us a sense of freedom to explore and experiment within the play's text without inhibition or contrivance. I had also found this to be true of my collaborations with Sonny Jim, a continuum of the New Lafayette aesthetic. This freedom allowed us to discover the heart of Matt's play and the spirit of Lincoln Perry with remarkable ease, the most difficult part being the memorization of an hour and ten minutes' worth of words, something I would imagine to be true for any actor performing a one-character monologue.

One of the most enjoyable and surprising aspects of Perry's character for me, besides his supremely infectious sense of humor, was his dancing prowess. Having begun his career as a song and dance man in touring shows throughout the South, he was famous for his fancy footwork long before his much wider success as a comic movie actor. Billy and I brought in my friend Hank Smith to help us "re-create" the colorful dance routines of Perry's early career, such as the "Jacksonville Juke," the "Corn Liquor Lulu," the "Knock-kneed Sally," and the pivotal "Step and Fetch It" from which the famous stage name would evolve. Hank, a television stage manager with whom I'd worked for years on *Sesame Street*, was also a longtime student and practitioner of traditional genres of African-American dance, including tap, soft-shoe, cake-walk, etc., and he relished the idea of reviving, based solely upon their names, the distinctive styles referred to in the play.

Wynn suggested and we agreed to hire set designer Kurt Lundell, with whom I had last worked on *House Party*, to create the simple but striking set for the play. The ever reliable Judy Dearing, by now one of the busiest and most respected costume designers in the business, captured the sharp contrast between the slovenly Fetchit and the dapper Perry. Robert LaPierre was brought on board by Billy to create a sound design of both vintage music and incidental sounds recorded and then cued alongside the lighting design of the wonderful Shirley Prendergast. Billy orchestrated the blending of these designs within the action and text of the play to seamless perfection, which, when aided by the expertise and dedication of the most crucial team member, production stage manager Jacqui Casto, resulted in the creation of a mesmerizing, hysterical, poignant, and extremely informative experience for our audience.

As for my own work, it was certainly among the best of my career, encompassing as full a spectrum of discipline and movement, both physically and emotionally, as anything I've done. In performing the character of Lincoln Perry I had the challenge of capturing a forceful, highly intelligent, and complex personality as well as that of displaying his formidable comic talents. The dual nature of the role allowed me to "show off" my gifts of mimicry, character acting, and storytelling in a multi-faceted and dazzling display of my craft. The critical establishment seemed to agree. From the first previews in late March, theater reviewers began trickling in to see the performance and, almost unanimously, applauded the show's unique blend of hilarity, poignancy, and biting commentary on America's and Hollywood's racial legacy. *New York Newsday*'s Jan Stuart wrote, *"In a superbly loose-limbed double performance, Roscoe Orman slips back and forth between the snail-brained Fetchit and the dapper, robustly alert Perry. The alternation has a deliberately unsettling effect, suspending us between alarm at Fetchit's antics and empathy for Perry's choices."* D. J. R. Bruckner of the *New York Times* concurred, *"Portraying a gifted performer is a tough assignment for an actor. Here, Roscoe Orman brings it off in style. Starting out with an hilarious typical Stepin Fetchit scene and going on to recall Perry's career and his fate as a rejected symbol of shame, Mr. Orman presents a man who grows larger and more troubling by the minute."* And Clive Barnes of the *New York Post* raved, *"The real success of this production is Orman's ability to step in and out of caricature and reality and to force us to realize almost painfully that when we make Fetchit and the roles he played into an Uncle Tom figure of contempt we are telling more about the America he lived in (and ourselves) than about dear old Stepin Fetchit."*

Despite such praise, however, the production had its detractors, although mostly among people who hadn't seen the performance but objected to the very notion of Perry's being given recognition as anything other than an object of ridicule and disgrace. I was somewhat confounded and saddened by such reactions, especially when coming from people for whom I'd had a measure of respect. Billie Allen, the talented

With Bill Lathan on opening night of THE CONFESSIONS OF STEPIN FETCHIT, American Place Theatre, 1993.

actress and director with whom I had performed in *Every Night When the Sun Goes Down* and who also served as an American Place Theatre board member, after first castigating Wynn Handman for having the audacity to produce a play about a man who remains "such an embarrassment to black people," refused to attend a performance despite Wynn's pleas. Ironically, the brand of hypocrisy and inequity that is so powerfully illuminated in the play has, in its modern-day embodiment, victimized black female artists like Ms. Allen more than almost any other group. The list of brilliant African-American women whose acting careers have been marginalized, held at bay, or totally thwarted by the industry would fill a book. Equally troubling to me were the responses of those like old friends Richard and Valerie Wesley and others who came to see the show and, seemingly, enjoyed it but also made it abundantly clear during the post-play discussion that they were profoundly offended by our attempt to absolve Perry of his selfish "crimes" against his people.

As Lincoln Perry in THE CONFESSIONS OF STEPIN FETCHIT, Luna Stage, 2006. (Courtesy of E.J. Carr.)

Within those same discussions, however, the play received a plethora of resounding endorsements, including those from such notable figures as United States Congressman Charles B. Rangel, as well as author and TV journalist Roger Rosenblatt, who later wrote *"To understand the character of Stepin Fetchit is to grasp the full extent of the joy and tragedy of Black Life in America. Roscoe Orman's portrayal of this hilarious, accusing, heartbreaking man is one of the most beautiful and instructive things ever to appear on stage,"* and legendary jazz drummer Max Roach, who chided white audiences and America in general for their duplicity. He accused whites of first derisively reveling at the antics of Stepin Fetchit (laughing for reasons quite different from those of the black working class audience who were very much aware and appreciative of the slyly subversive nature of Perry's buffoonery) and then conveniently joining in the chorus of his condemnation so as to allay their feelings of guilt for having enjoyed him in the first place.

Given both the powerful response to the play and its provocative nature it became obvious to Billy and me that we had created an exceptionally entertaining, incendiary, and informative piece of theater which deserved a longer life. The play seemed to strike a nerve within the consciousness of our audiences, tapping into an area of what I consider to be the "unfinished business" of reconciling parts of our unspeakably painful past with an increasingly complex modern existentialist society. The contradictions which are still deeply embedded within the American psyche in regards to racial matters warrant our persistent attention to the subject and to its long and tortured history. The story of Lincoln Perry as told in Matt's play contained these and all of the horrifying disparities inherent within America's treatment of its citizens of African descent.

Consequently, my commitment to *The Confessions of Stepin Fetchit* extended well beyond its short run at American Place Theatre. After a failed attempt to secure financing for a commercial run based upon the play's critical success, together with Billy and Jacqui, and with Matt's approval, I decided to explore the possibilities of touring the piece on the college and regional theater circuit. Agent Paul Jacob and I put together a promotional package and began to book engagements for the play to be performed at several of such locations, including LeMoyne College in Syracuse, the University of Southern Illinois, San Rafael Jewish Community Center in northern California, St. Louis Black Repertory Company, Smithsonian Institution in Washington D.C., Atlanta's National Black Arts Festival, and others.

The response of audiences at each of these venues to both the play and its follow-up discussions resonated deeply with a sense of the subject's importance to a generation hungering for historical meaning and context. It was a revelation for me to discover the multitude of unanswered questions which still reside within the hearts and minds of a nation whose racial history has been steeped in shame and denial. Most encouraging was my newfound perception of Americans as a people with an enormous hidden capacity to discuss, learn, change, and grow. Thus began what has become both a perpetual showcase and a kind of crusade in which I get to practice the craft which I've spent a lifetime mastering and, at the same time, offer an important lesson in the cultural history of our nation. Given the ageless quality of Perry (and his alter ego) and his actual longevity in life, I could, and hope to, periodically revive this piece for the remainder of my career much in the same way that Hal Holbrook has done with his celebrated incarnation of the great Mark Twain.

With acting great Jose Ferrer.

Solana and me with Yolanda King. (Photo by Gideon Mannasseh.)

Backstage with the wonderful Mary Alice, 1997.

With Julianne Moore.

With Gordon Parks.
(Photo by Kojo Ade.)

With Alicia Keys.
(Photo by Nikki Parker.)

With Bill and Hillary Clinton at the White House.

Celebrating Cookie's 60th with Leslie and Cookie, 2005.

With best buddy Tommy Hicks at Rose Bowl, 2004.

CHAPTER THIRTEEN
Regeneration

Ripened Heart

Hearts beat deep with age
Unlike pitter-patter carefree youth
Whose indiscreet delights belie the truth
Of two young lovers' souls
Whose devotion so complete,
So sweet the touch of new love yet untried
Unencumbered by the ache of weary feet
Whose travails will bury furrows deep inside
The heart so steeped in age.
The sage embodies memories in the limbs
Which guide the soul to wiser love
Above the wasteful whims that early life demands.
Old hands have learned to hold, to mold,
Caress the fragile pulse of treasured life,
Love's resting place, the well-fed face of bounty.
And count the blessings harvested by such,
This heart so full in age
So full of all that time has wrought, its lessons
Caught in space, its pains erased by measured grace
And placed where they belong,
In oblivion.

11/11/05

Ironically, during this period of heightened artistic fulfillment derived from *The Confessions of Stepin Fetchit*, in the area of career management things were far from ideal and rapidly deteriorating. The Ambrosio/Mortimer Agency, with whom I had experienced both good and not so good moments, began to have serious difficulties which seemed to stem mostly from Lou Ambrosio's underhanded dealings, resulting in a severe lack of credibility both among the agency's clientele and within the industry at large. A class action lawsuit was eventually filed on behalf of those clients who may have been victims of fraud. Fortunately for me, except for a bounced check early on in our relationship (which was immediately replaced), I had not, to my knowledge, suffered any direct losses, but the ordeal of losing yet another agent, one whom I had hoped would accelerate my career, was distressing, to say the least.

Despite this misfortune and the extraordinary nature of my experiences with Matt's play, the events surrounding my professional life were, once again, upstaged by a major family occurrence. Conceived shortly after the run at American Place and born the following winter, Sharon's and my fourth child, Cheyenne Delores Orman, brought her angelic spirit into our lives on February 10, 1994, thus completing an arc of procreation and child rearing that had begun nearly twenty years earlier. Unlike most families with multiple children (rare in itself these days), each of our four were born at least four and a half years apart, and, in the case of Miles and Cheyenne, were separated by more than nine years.

This was far from accidental. Early on, Sharon and I had agreed to space our children in such a way so as to allow each of them a full period of pre-school nurturing devoid of the intense rivalry common among sibling toddlers. The first three to five years of life, it seemed to us, were so crucial to a child's development that, ideally, there should be as much time and attention as possible devoted to each during these years. In observing other parents with two or three (and even four) children all under school age, the level of stress and demand on both parents and children seemed to prohibit the optimum emotional and psychological growth for all. My long experience in relating to children through my work on *Sesame Street* has taught me valuable lessons about how to appreciate the special qualities of early childhood development when approached with joy and relaxation and ample time to relate and interact.

I also knew from my own childhood the special kind of appreciation that one can have for a much younger sibling, such as I had (and still do) for my sister Leslie, twelve years my junior, and brother Pancho, who was born when I was seventeen. Having Pancho around, in fact, offered me an early "dry run" experience at some of the peripheral duties of parenthood as well as a better understanding of the deeper levels of responsibility attached to it. Although there is probably an equally good argument to be made for the unique bond among siblings close in age, Sharon and I preferred the longer, slower path, one of the many benefits of which is the level of expertise that one can acquire (if one has the stamina) after a few decades of experience in child rearing. Rasheda's younger siblings have certainly benefited from what she taught Sharon and me as young parents about patience, control, and allowing nature to take its course.

Of course, for me, all of the normally expected joys of parenthood have been greatly enhanced by the unexpected turn that my career path took thirty years ago. The ability to share the essence and character of my work, both literally and figuratively, with each of my four children has been an incomparable delight, creating a special unspoken bond between me and them which endures. The periodic critiques that each of them has given me over the years regarding my appearances in various films, plays, and other television shows have been a mix of everything from raves to mild approvals to outright pans, but *Sesame Street* (even to Solana, the least enthusiastic of the four) has always held a special place in their hearts. The fact that they have each appeared on the show has given them a certain sense of ownership and empowerment in addition to the universal appeal that *Sesame Street* has held for millions of children over several generations. The addition of Cheyenne to this family tradition has, especially as I enter my seventh decade of existence (and my fourth of being Gordon), given unexpected new vitality and meaning to my work on the show, instilling within me an even deeper appreciation of the direction that this uncommon path has bestowed upon my life.

Despite the above, it should be noted that the evolution of *Sesame Street* in its form, its content, and its prominence over the past decade has had its share of challenge and uncertainty. For many years the unrivaled champion of children's programming, with near unanimous recognition as such, *Sesame Street*'s predominance has, in recent years, been contested by a multitude of "new kids on the block." It began with the advent of *Barney* in the early 1990s, a show that reversed and repudiated nearly every characteristic which had endeared *Sesame Street* to millions of preschoolers, parents, and educators for 25 years. Simplistic in its aims and its level of production, *Barney* appealed to a younger audience than ours with its "cutesy" style of performance, its antiseptic atmosphere, its blatantly derivative music (*"I love you"/"This old man"*), and its huge commercial marketing campaign preceding the show's premiere. *Barney*, of course, was just another example of the general "dumbing down" of American popular culture within the last twenty years exemplified further by the abundance of degradingly sensationalistic "talk," "court," and "reality" shows permeating the airwaves today. Within its first few seasons, *Barney* had taken a big bite out of our audience share and signaled to the television industry that there was an enormous untapped market for children's entertainment that need not be so high-minded as *Sesame Street* or *Mister Rogers' Neighborhood* (a production which, due to the unwavering integrity of its creator and star Fred Rogers, has always eschewed commercialism in favor of social and moral responsibility).

When *Sesame Street* first appeared on the airwaves in pre-cable 1969, television audiences could choose from among only three networks, a smattering of local stations, and the fledgling Public Broadcasting System. Over the last fifteen years, there has been a virtual explosion of new children's programming, culminating in the creation of Nickelodeon, Cartoon Network, The Disney Channel, and other cable stations devoted exclusively to shows for kids. Programs such as *Rugrats, Hey Arnold, Blue's Clues, Dora the Explorer, SpongeBob SquarePants, Ginger, Nick News, Little Bill, Bear in the Big Blue House, Scooby Doo Where Are You?, Cat Dog, Powerpuff Girls,* and others, began to dominate children's viewing habits, leading CTW (recently renamed Sesame Workshop) and its newly assembled creative team to explore the need for change in the look, feel, and content of our show.

One of the more significant (and to my mind regrettable) of these changes has been the gradually diminishing presence of the adult humans on the show as consistent and reassuring figures of authority. In past years our prominence had served as a counterbalance to the population of Muppets like Big Bird, Snuffleupagus, Grover, Cookie Monster, and others who constantly looked to us for our gentle and dependable guidance. In more recent years Muppet pre-schoolers such as Elmo, Zoe, Baby Bear, Telly, and their friends, although still occasionally aided by advice from Bob, Susan, Luis, Maria, or Gordon, have increasingly resided in a world of their own, devoid of a steady diet of grownup supervision. This is, of course, very much in line with the general landscape of children's television in which parents and other authority figures, if they exist at all, are often either peripheral in nature or objects of ridicule, or both. Despite (or perhaps, because of) its adjustments to these and other demands of the new marketplace, *Sesame Street* has had to gradually relinquish its once dominant position in the battle for ratings (a battle that didn't even exist during the show's early years) and, as a result, substantially reduce its production load from an original 130 shows to 100 to 85 to 50 to its currently scheduled 26 shows per season. Whatever the future may hold for *Sesame Street* and for those of us who have devoted so much of our lives to its creation and growth, we all should feel an enormous sense of pride in what the show has meant to an entire generation of world citizens whose gratitude and affection have been a continual affirmation to us.

One of the most important facets of the *Sesame Street* legacy has been its groundbreaking vision of inclusion. Long before the current mantra of cultural diversity became a popular catch phrase in America, *Sesame Street's* producers embraced the challenge of creating a model from which our children could create a future society based upon a knowledge and appreciation of others. The shining image of this neighborhood which contains every conceivable type of humanity all living in an atmosphere of harmony and respect has gestated and matured within the hearts and minds of an entire generation. This is true to such an extent that often the depth of response from among our older fans when they encounter us is beyond their capacity to understand. Our appearance on the *Sesame Street* float in the Macy's Thanksgiving Day Parade for each of the past 30 or so years is a prime example. As we all, Muppets and humans alike, ride down the parade route from the Museum of Natural History on West 79th Street to Macy's Department Store on West 34th, the unanimous eruption of cheers and the faces of unbridled delight (often tear-drenched) from both young and old speak volumes about the deep connection we and our program have established with millions of men, women, and children across the globe.

No less important or meaningful to me has been the continuation of my theatrical career over these four decades. I cannot overemphasize the level of spiritual sustenance that I have drawn from the body of work accumulated over these years and also from the scores of friendships and professional bonds which have continued to inspire and motivate me. Since *The Confessions of Stepin Fetchit*, I have performed in Woodie King, Jr.'s 1997 revival of James De Jongh's powerful slave narrative drama *Do Lord Remember Me* at Manhattan's Sylvia and Danny Kaye Playhouse with an all-star cast featuring Ebony Jo-Ann, Glynn Turman, Barbara Montgomery, and Chuck Patterson. Originally produced twenty years earlier at the New Federal The-

With Glynn Turman, Robert Townsend, and Ebony. Jo-Ann at Do Lord Remember Me opening night, 1997.

atre, *Do Lord* was based on actual reminiscences collected in the 1930s of African-Americans who had been born into slavery. The act of portraying this collection of octogenarians whose lives had contained episodes of nearly inconceivable brutality, endurance, and triumph was like an exercise in spirit channeling for each of us in the cast. The outstanding ensemble work of this splendid company under the direction of Regge Life was honored with an AUDELCO Award, giving me my first win after five nominations.

Later that summer, with Lou Myers replacing Chuck Patterson, *Do Lord* was included as part of the National Black Theatre Festival (NBTF) in Winston-Salem, North Carolina, offering me my first exposure to this brilliantly conceived and wonderfully executed week-long celebration of the theater arts. My introduction to the NBTF was truly a revelation. The genius of festival founder and director Larry Leon Hamlin lay in his ability to create an amalgamation which included a grassroots affiliation of theater companies from across the country and around the globe, major corporate and regional public support and, finally, the largest and most celebrated collection of black theater artists ever assembled in one place to both perform and give endorsement to the event; *and* to repeat this every two years. I was astounded by the depth and breadth of this accomplishment and was also thrilled to be reunited with and introduced to scores of fellow artists from both coasts and the regions in between. What *if*, I couldn't help but wonder, what if Hamlin or someone like him had been around back during the "golden age" of black theater activity in the seventies? Perhaps some of those companies that prematurely folded would have been given the level of promotional support they needed to survive that period. We'll never know.

Larry Hamlin subsequently invited me back to the NBTF in 1999 to perform *The Confessions of Stepin Fetchit*, which became one of the highlights of that year's festival offerings. Just as I had anticipated, the festival provided the ideal audience for a play about the life and career of a performing pioneer, albeit one whose legacy continues to perplex and conflict many among us. The outpouring of love, respect, and encouragement I received from a broad spectrum of my colleagues, especially people like Lincoln Kilpatrick, Ed Cambridge, Lex Monson, Robert Hooks, and others who had been among my career's early role models, was extremely gratifying.

Also during this period of the mid-to-late 1990s I worked on two independent film projects with the talented Jamal Joseph, screenwriter, director, and husband to acting colleague Joyce Walker (Joseph). The first was an original tele-drama of Jamal's entitled *Drive-By*. Shot entirely on location in Harlem, the film tells the fact-based story of an inner-city mother (played by Joyce) who shackles her teenage son to his bed in order to prevent him from pursuing activities which would have inevitably led to his demise, thereby saving his life. *Drive-By* is a heartfelt plea to parents and society in general to take seriously the responsibility we have for the protection of our young. In it, I play Pops, the proprietor of a local teen hangout who assists the mother in her efforts to corral her son's behavior. In a similar vein, Jamal's next directorial effort *Cross the Line* (originally titled *Full Court Press*), an as-yet-unreleased independent feature written and produced by motivational entrepreneur Roger Flax and filmed in northern New Jersey, tackles the subject of racial conflict and insensitivity between black and white teens. Among the performers in the film were such notable talents as Hill Harper, Ellen Burstyn, Kim Staunton, Taye Diggs, O.L. Duke, and rap star Da Brat. I played the part of JoJo Barnes, a conscientious and charitable community-based business man who is a mentor and father figure to the younger generation.

The following year during the summer of 1997, I spent four weeks in lovely Wilmington, North Carolina (hometown of Michael Jordan), shooting *Sesame Street*'s long-awaited second feature film *The Adventures of Elmo in Grouchland*. It had been thirteen years since the making of *Follow That Bird* and this was a rare chance in recent years for us cast members to spend some quality time together outside the studio's confines. In addition to our entire company, the movie also included cameo appearances by the versatile performers Mandy Patinkin and Vanessa L. Williams. Like *Bird*, this film involved the loss and subsequent search and rescue of one of the beloved Muppet children, in this case the precociously adorable Elmo. Produced by Brian Henson and directed by

Vanessa L. Williams, her son Devin Hervey, and I relax during shooting of THE ADVENTURES OF ELMO IN GROUCHLAND. (Courtesy of Betty Lou Skinner.)

Hollywood TV veteran Gary Halvorson, *Elmo in Grouchland* provided yet another showcase for the formidable talents of Elmo's alter-ego Kevin Clash, who also served as the film's executive producer. Over the previous decade, Kevin, *Sesame Street*'s Muppet captain, had elevated the little furry red monster to superstar status both on the show (*Elmo's World*) and in the world-at-large (frequent talk-show guest, the subject of best selling doll Tickle-Me-Elmo, and two primetime specials *Elmopalooza* and *Elmo Saves Christmas*). Particularly interesting and impressive is the fact that Kevin also happens to be the only African-American performer among the Henson Muppeteers working on the show.

More recently, I made a long overdue return to the world of regional theater for the Madison Repertory Theatre's 2002 production of *Fences*. The theater's directors, D. Scott Glasser and Tony Foreman, offered me the role of the play's towering protagonist Troy Maxson at their Civic Center facility in lovely and hospitable Madison, Wisconsin. This production of what I consider to be August Wilson's masterpiece, sensitively directed by fellow South Bronx native Shirley Basfield Dunlap with an exceptional cast made up of mostly Chicago-based actors, was the first of a Wilson play to be presented by this highly reputable Midwestern company. The quality of the presentation was exceptional and the audience's response to it could not have been better. I had great fun during my six weeks of working with fellow cast members D.J. Howard, Vikki J. Myers, Karim Ra (Ferguson), Clifton Williams, Herbert Parker, and little Brittany Habermehl. It was especially gratifying for me to finally perform a role that I consider to be one of the most compelling and challenging in modern theater, one which I had dreamed of playing since my first encounter with the play on Broadway some fourteen years earlier. Troy's brave, tenacious, and exasperating struggle with his demon-filled past, his rich depth of character and gifts of storytelling, his athleticism and charisma, and the powerful resonance of his family's legacy propelled me into new realms of theatrical expression.

In the remaining arc of my career, I intend to expand upon these past forty years of work in theater, film, and television. To a large degree, I still consider myself to be a student of the craft which has taught me many things about life and the art of living. The various stages upon which I've had the privilege of working have provided me with venues of learning, laboratories, universities, and temples of knowledge from which I have and continue to glean much about life's meanings. Extensive as my forty years of experience may be, I still see myself as very much a work in progress and feel that I have but scratched the surface of the mother lode of creativity within me. Obviously, as is true with life itself, age and experience, when given their due, can add immeasurably to the quality and dimension of one's work. Consequently, it is my sincere hope, intention, and belief that the highest of my career's accomplishments and its true crowning glory have yet to be achieved.

As I enter and begin to reside within the realm of the elders, I hope to reflect well upon the best of those who have preceded me, especially those whose contributions have been overlooked, dimin-

With D.J. Howard and Vikki J. Myers in FENCES, Madison Repertory Theatre, 2002.

ished, or denied. The legacies of the many gifted and courageous souls whose lives have enriched us demand that we whose spirits they have nourished take up the task of advancing the cause of human progress in their names. This inter-generational reciprocity, vis-à-vis my elders as well as with the younger breed, has immeasurably deepened the meaning of my life's journey. The catastrophic events of 9/11/01 and their aftermath have brought into even sharper focus the fragility and the sanctity of all life and the imperative need for each of us to fulfill our life's purpose, whatever it may be.

In the course of writing this book I have also discovered new meanings in the ongoing dialogue which reverberates around the themes of my own personal tale. In recounting the episodes of my journey, time has been condensed, reshaped, or obliterated and much of what is long past has been made to seem recent. A synthesis of all the various parts of me has created a whole new understanding of who and what I have become. The small boy with a speech impediment who sang to his kindergarten class about *That Lucky Ole Sun*; the student sit-in protester who bemoans the *Lovin' and Hatin' Blues* of racism; the young idealist who confronts a *World Full of Gray* and begs for *Opportunity to Please Knock*; the prodigal son who returns home to stand at his father's coffin and affirm himself as one *Whose Got His Own*; the blindly ambitious *Dynamite* pimp who is forced to see the terrible error of his ways; the former radical and member of *The Talented Tenth* who now, as corporate climber, must crash and burn at mid-life to start again; the strikingly talented, celebrated, but infamous entertainer, groundbreaker, and Hollywood icon who comes back from the grave to *Confess* and assert his legacy; and, of course, the husband, father, teacher, and friend who looks to the needs of all the residents on his famous *Street* and is loved for it by generations of young viewers; they and a multitude of others all commingle within my soul as metaphors and as tangible components of myself and the world that I have known. Their myriad songs of redemption, renewal, learning, and growth continue to accompany my dreams, to inform and inspire me in my pursuit of humanity's highest and most life-affirming goals.

In closing, let me state that the events as recalled and recounted in these pages represent a faithful rendering of occurrences as I have experienced and seen them. Although human memory over time is inevitably subject to some natural imperfections, omissions, and emphases, I have not consciously misrepresented myself or the incidents described herein and sincerely hope that for the reader my story will make palpable the true spirit and meaning of that which is depicted. I also hope that those others who have participated in this story and survive will concur in the faithfulness of my efforts and share with me in the joy of giving substance to the collective experience of our past. To those participants who are no longer among us I offer tribute and reaffirmation of their contribution to my life's journey. May theirs and all our spirits continue to live through the memories and the deeds of those who remain among the living.

Index List

Abraham, Naji Mulia 59
ACLU (American Civil Liberties Union) 33
Actors' Equity Association (AEA) 19, 93
Actors Studio 17, 21, 48, 49, 102
Adderley, Julian "Cannonball" 15
Adderley, Nat 15, 104
Adu, Frank 100, 108
Adventures of Elmo in Grouchland, The 191
Afro-American Studio for Acting and Speech 61, 68
Ailey, Alvin 14
Albee, Edward 21
Alda, Alan 75
Aldridge, Ira 166, 170
Alexander, Brooks 56
Ali, Muhammad 30, 35
Ali, Tatyana 152
Alice, Mary 64, 108, 110, 152, 180
All My Children 93-94
Allen, Billie 22, 100, 177
Alston, Barbara 99
Ambrosio, Lou 167, 172, 185
American Place Theatre 49, 53-54, 64, 100, 106, 174, 177, 179
American Program Bureau (APB) 105-106
Andrisano, Tommy 15
Angelou, Maya 23, 76, 127
Aranha, Ray 152
Arieta, Gil 15
Arkin, Alan 21

Armstrong, Louis 171
Astor, Richard 100, 149, 166-167
AUDELCO Awards 100, 122, 190
Ayers-Allen, Phylicia 84-85, 121
Ayler, Ethel 23

Babatunde, Akin 100
Babatunde, Obba 100
Baker, Josephine 166
Baldwin, James 29, 33, 166
Balin, Richard 19
Baraka, Amiri (LeRoi Jones) 22-23, 58, 65, 67-68, 74
Barnes, Clive 176
Barnes, Marjorie 84
Barnes, Verona 64
Barnette, M. Neema 65, 156
Bartlett (O'Reilly), Alison 91, 130, 146, 164
Bass, Kingsley B. 58
Bassett, Angela 143, 153, 167
Baxter, Karen Allen vii, 66, 154
Bearden, Romare 64
Belafonte, Harry 29-30, 127
Belgrave, Cynthia 22, 107
Benjamin, Paul 112
Bennett, Tony 20
Benson, George 127
Benson, Robbie 168
Berry, Kelly-Marie 54
Best, Willie 171
Bevel, James 30
Bey, Chief 59
Bey, Marki 100

Biondo, Frankie 126
Black Arts Repertory Theatre/School 58, 68
Black Panther Party 37, 40, 53, 64
Black Theatre Magazine 65
Black Troupe 64
Boseman, Jesse 67
Bogalusa Story, The 37
Bogart, Humphrey 77
Bolling, Gary vii, 22, 24, 48, 51, 54, 56, 64, 158
Bond, Julian 30
Bosia, Akosua 155
Boudraux, Mel 121
Bourne, St. Clair vii, 151
Bove, Linda 91, 96, 130, 146, 164
Brand, Phoebe 48
Breaking Light 120
Brecht, Bertolt 36-37, 42
Brill, Fran 126, 130
Bringing Up Jack 168
Brooks, Avery 108, 111, 155
Brooks, Gwendolyn 14
Brown, Bryan 149
Brown, Charles 111, 152
Brown, David 74, 79
Brown, Graham 84, 158
Brown, Johnny Mack 77
Brown, Oscar, Jr. 14, 27-28
Browne, Roscoe Lee 23, 106
Bruckner, D.J.R. 176
Bullard, Tom 101-102
Bullins, Ed 51, 53, 55-58, 60, 63-65, 68, 100
Bullock, Elden 121
Burnett, Charles 79
Burrows, Vinie 23
Burstyn, Ellen 191
Bush, Barbara 127, 129-131, 137
Bush, Norman 22, 24, 51

Butts, Reverend Calvin 156
Buzzi, Ruth 130

Cagney, James 77
Caldwell, Ben 65
Caldwell, L. Scott 111, 153, 168
Calloway, Northern 91, 96
Cambridge, Godfrey 23
Campbell, Lydia 10
Camus, Albert 58
Candy, John 127
Cannon, Reuben 76
Cardinal Hayes High School 12-13
Cardwell, Carolyn 14
Carmen Jones 14
Carmichael, Bruce "Khalil" 59
Carmichael, Stokely 30, 34, 40
Carnovsky, Morris 48, 118
Carroll, Diahann 15
Carter, Rosanna 55, 64
Carter, Steve 84
Casado, Desiree 126
Casey, Bernie 80
Cash, Rosalind 51, 80, 112
Cassidy, Hopalong 77
Castle, Oretha 43
Casto, Jacqui 176, 178
Cerf, Chris 126
Chaikin, Joseph 48
Charles, Martie 66
Charles, Ray 126-127, 145
Chipkin, Leo 18, 29
Chipkin, Paul 18, 28, 29
Chisolm, Earl 28
Christian, Robert 107-108
Christmas Eve on Sesame Street 105
Circle in the Square Theatre School 16-17, 31, 70
Clanton, Rony 22, 156
Clara's Ole Man 53, 63

SESAME STREET DAD | 197

Clark, Juanita 122
Clarke, Barbara 121
Clash, Kevin 138, 192
Clinton, Bill 182
Clinton, Hillary Rodham 127, 130-131, 182
Clooney, Rosemary 127
Close, Glenn 127
Clurman, Harold 118
Cobb, Charlie 43
Cobbs, Bill 150, 158
Coleman, Marilyn 78
Collins, Beverly 51, 56
Collins, Richard 18
Collins, Rise 107
Collins, Rufus 17
Colon, Miriam 108
Confessions of Stepin Fetchit, The 169-179, 185, 189-190
Connell, Dave 86
Conover, Grandin 48
Conrad, Robert 120
Cook, Peter 21
Cooney, Joan Ganz 4, 91, 95, 131
Cooper, Lee 104
Copeland, Maurice 107
Cordier, Robert 32, 37
Coriolanus 107-110
Cosby, Bill 15, 95
Costley, Robert "Big Daddy" 31, 38
Cox, Courtland 12, 30
Cross the Line 191
Cruse, Harold 52
Curtis, Norman 13-16, 27-28
Curtis, Patricia Taylor 13-16, 20, 27
Cutler, Ron 74

Da Brat 191
DaCosta, Jose 73
DaCosta, Lucille 73

Dandridge, Dorothy 14, 30
Dara, Olu 151
Davidson, John 19
Davis, Ossie 19, 107, 156, 169
Day, Cora Lee 74, 76, 141-142, 172-173
Deacons for Defense and Justice 37-38
Dean, Philip Hayes 68, 100, 174
Dee, Ruby 29, 106-107, 156, 169
Dearing, Judy 84, 102, 176
De Jongh, James 174, 189
Delgado, Emilio 91, 96, 130, 146, 159, 164
Dennehy, Brian 149
Dent, Tom 40, 133
Devil Catchers, The 57, 60
Devine, Loretta 104
De Young, Cliff 149
Diego, Ken 126
Diggs, Taye 191
DiNapoli, Victor 126
Dinkins, David 138
Does Man Help Man? 42
Do Lord Remember Me 174, 189
Donahue, Phil 127
Donaldson, Lou 12
Donaldson, Lydia 12
Donaldson, Norma 78
Downing, David 51, 86
Drive-By 191
Duberman, Martin 36, 37
DuBois, W.E.B. xii, 166
Duke, Bill 64, 79, 99, 143
Duke, O.L. 191
Duma, Ndlovu 154
Dunlap, Shirley Basfield 192
Duplex, The 57, 60, 121
DuPois, Starletta 64, 102
Dutton, Charles S. 152, 167, 170

Duvall, Robert 22
Dylan, Bob 29

Earley, Candice 93
Edelman, Marian Wright 133
Edwards, Gloria 99
Edwards, Gus 103
Electric Company, The 91, 163
Electronic Nigger, The 53-54, 109
Ellington, Duke 20, 57
Ellis, Helen 48, 51, 54, 56, 58, 64
Elie, Lolis 43
Eliot, Marge 100
Emmy Awards 164
Enter Laughing 19, 21
Erving, Julius 127
Evans, Dale 77
Evans, Don 103
Evans, Estelle 49-51, 54, 56
Evening of African & Afro-American Poetry, An 42
Every Night When the Sun Goes Down 100, 174, 177

Fabulous Miss Marie, The 57, 60, 121
Faison, Frankie 108, 111, 151
Faison, Olamide 126
Fantastiks, The 19
Fargas, Antonio 22, 24
Fayed, Dodi 149
Fences 152-154, 192
Fenner, Janice 50
Fernandez, Peter Jay 108
Ferrer, Jose 127, 180
Fetchit, Stepin 170-173, 176, 178
Fierstein, Harvey 100
Fillmore East 64, 141
Fishburne, Lawrence 143
Five Blind Boys of Alabama 153

Flax, Roger 191
Follow That Bird 143, 191
Ford, Clebert 23, 99, 108, 121-122
Ford Foundation 56
Foreman, Tony 192
Forman, James 30
Foster, Frances 51, 104, 150
Foster, Gloria 108-109
Foxx, Redd 93, 142
Franciosa, Tony 75-76
Frank, Miss (5th grade teacher) 11
Frankel, Gene 47
Franklin, Carl 75, 79, 143
Frazier, Sheila 80
Frederick, Mrs. (kindergarten teacher) 10
Freeman, Al, Jr. 22, 84
Freeman, Morgan 101, 108, 110, 120-121, 143, 153, 163, 166
Free Southern Theater (FST) xii, 27-32, 34, 36-43, 47, 49, 61, 65, 74-75, 118, 169, 174
French, Arthur 99, 107-108, 121
Freudberg, Judy 126
Full Court Press 191
Fuller, Charles 68
F/X 149, 154, 166

Gaines, Sonny Jim 51, 55-56, 70, 108, 110, 121, 122, 156, 158, 168
Gallagher, Jack 168
Gant, Richard 101, 154, 156-157
Gardner, Rob 164
Geiss, Tony 126
Genet, Jean 23
Gibbons, Lana (cousin) 12, 73
Gibson, Hoot 77
Gielgud, John 109
Gillespie, Dizzy 127

Glasser, D. Scott 192
Glover, Danny 143
Glover, Savion 91, 146
Goin'a Buffalo 60, 63, 121
Goldberg, Whoopi 127, 143
Gordon, Carl 99
Gordy, Denise 78
Gossett, Louis, Jr. 23, 48
Gottfried, Martin 102
Graham, Elain 156
Great MacDaddy, The 84, 86, 158
Greene, Loretta 85
Grice, Wayne 54
Grimes, Nicholas 19
Grifasi, Joe 149
Guillaume, Robert 87
Guinness, Alec 22
Gunn, Moses 23, 51

Habermehl, Brittany 193
Hagen, Uta 17, 21
Haley, Alex 40
Hall, Albert 78, 99
Hamlin, Larry Leon 190
Handman, Wynn 53, 64, 100, 106, 174, 177
Hansberry, Lorraine 14, 16, 75
Hard Time on Planet Earth 154, 168
Hardy, William 104
Harewood, Al 59, 64
Harewood, Dorian 102
Harper, Hill 191
Harris, Neal 121-122
Harrison, Paul Carter 68, 84
Halvorson, Gary 192
Hawkins, Emalyn 31
Hawkins, Yvette 14, 51, 55-56, 101, 103
Hayes, Gabby 77
Hayes, Lori 121

Hayeson, Jimmy 99
Hemphill, Marcus 120
Henderson, David 12
Henderson, Luther 104
Hendry, Gloria 80
Henson, Brian 191
Henson, Jim 87, 95
Hicks, Tommy vii, 64, 121, 172, 182
High School of Art and Design (A&D) 13-15, 18
Hill, Arthur 21
Hill, Sam 42
Hill, Thelma 21
Hines, Gregory 127, 160
Hingle, Pat 21
Hockenhull, Ike 103, 170
Hoffman, Dustin 22, 174
Holbrook, Hal 179
Holder, Lawrence 170
Holly, Ellen 22, 106
Hooks, Bebe Drake 84
Hooks, Robert "Bobby Dean" 22, 51, 80, 184, 191
House Party 64, 100, 175
Howard, Bette 51, 55-56
Howard, D.J. 192-193
Howard, Ruth 43
How Do You Do? 64, 141
Howell, Bill 59
Hudlin brothers 79
Hughes brothers 79
Hughes, Kate 75
Hughes, Langston 16, 29, 151, 166
Hunt, Richard 127
Hurd, Hugh 101
Hurston, Zora Neale 166, 170
Hyman, Earl 64, 108

If We Grow Up 14, 16, 18, 20, 29

Innis, Roy 52
In the Wine Time 53, 56-57
In White America 36, 39
I Speak of Africa 42

Jackson, Leonard (L. Errol Jaye) 54, 108-110, 152
Jackson, Mahalia 103-104
Jackson, Michael 144
Jackson, Samuel L. 143, 166-167
Jacksons, The 144
Jacob, Norman 36
Jacob, Paul 106, 179
Jamal, Sati 84
James, Gary vii, 64
James, Peter Francis 108
Jaroslow, Ruth 19
Jay, William 51, 108
Jennings, Brent 101
JoAnn, Ebony 189
Joffrey, Marissa 17, 31
Johnson, Bernard 76
Johnson, Jack xii
Johnson, J.J. 78
Johnson, Louis 56
Johnson, Lyndon 34
Johnson, Reginald Vel 108
Jones, James Earl 23, 106, 127, 152, 170
Jones, LeRoi *see* Baraka, Amiri
Jones, Robert Earl 78
Jonesboro Story, The 37
Jonsson, Judyann 51
Jordan, Michael 60, 191
Joseph, Jamal 191
Julia, Raul 106
Julien, Max 80
Julius Caesar 107
Judd, Robert 152
Just Assassins, The 58

Kahn, Michael 16-17, 19, 22-23, 64
Kain, Gylan 85, 108, 110
Kazan, Elia 17, 118
Kaufman, Fran 137, 139
Kay, Monte 15
Keiser, Kris 51, 54, 56
Keitel, Harvey 17
Kelly, Gene 29
Kennedy, Adrienne 22, 68
Kennedy, John F. 13, 27
Kerr, Herb 101, 121
Keys, Alicia 127, 181
Keyes, Joe 74
KidsDay 133
Kilpatrick, Lincoln 23, 191
Kilpatrick, Peggy 51, 55-56, 121
King, B.B. 127, 159
King, Dr. Martin Luther, Jr. 28-30, 33-34, 52, 55-56, 133
King, Woodie, Jr. 62, 69, 85, 103, 189
King, Yolanda 180
Kingsley, Emily 126
KKK (Ku Klux Klan) 37
Knight, Gladys 127, 145
Knight-Pulliam, Keisha 127
Kojak 93, 149
Kove, Martin 154
Kozak, Harley Jane 168
Krone, Gerald 51

LaBelle, Patti 105, 107, 159
Laine, Frankie 10
La Mama Experimental Theatre Club 62, 99
Langham, Michael 65, 107-110
LaRue, Lash 77
Last Street Play, The 101-102, 107, 118, 120, 156-158, 163

Lathan, Bill vii, 51, 55-56, 65, 70, 84-86, 168, 170, 177-179
Lathan, Stan 86, 154
Lawson, Richard 158
Leach, Wilford 107
Leaks, Sylvester 52
Lee, Spike 79, 127, 143, 166
Lee, Will 91, 96, 104, 118, 164
Leguizamo, John 169-170, 174
Lester, Noble Lee 121
Levinson, Gabriel 14
Levy, Murray 31-32
Lewis, Erik vii, 41
Lewis, Gil 103, 108
Lewis, John 104
Lewis, Victor 47
Liddy, G. Gordon 120
Life, Regge 65, 190
Lincoln, Abbe 15
Lindfors, Viveca 47
Lindo, Delroy 153
Little, Cleavon 84, 86
Lockhart, Calvin 80
Lombard, Rudy 43
Long, Loretta 4, 15, 91, 96, 104-105, 126, 130, 137-138, 145-146, 159, 164
Long, Peter 15
Longo, Cezare 20
Lowry, McNeil 56
Lucas, George 60
Lumbly, Carl 153
Lundell, Kurt 164, 175

Mabley, Jackie "Moms" 170
Macbeth, Robert 45-54, 56-57, 59, 61, 63-64, 67, 69-70, 86, 102, 151
Macbeth, Toby 44, 64, 67
Madison Repertory Theatre 192-193

Mahalia 103, 170
Man Called Hawk, A 155
Mandell, Robert 149, 154
Manhattan School of Music 20
Manhattan Theatre Club 85, 101-103, 106, 155
Mann, Theodore 16
Manzano, Sonia 91, 96, 104, 126, 130, 137, 146, 150, 159, 164
March on Washington, D.C. (1963) 28-29
Marcy, George 19
Marin, Cheech 127, 160
Marrow, Esther 103-104
Marshall, William 80
Marsalis, Branford 127
Marsalis, Wynton 127
Martin, D'Urville 22, 24
Martin, Helen 20
Martin, Jim 126
Matlock, Norman 100, 108
May, Ted 126
Maynard, Ken 77
Mayo, Whitman 51, 55-56, 66, 142, 172
McCarthy, Joseph 118
McCauley, Robbie 108
McClintock, Ernie 53, 61
McCoy, Tim 77
McCutcheon, Bill 91, 146
McDaniel, Hattie 171
McFerrin, Bobby 127
McGhee, Vonetta 80
McGill, Bruce 107
McGrath, Bob 91, 96, 104, 145-146, 159, 164
McIntyre, Diane 151
McLaughlin, David 32
McQueen, Butterfly 171
Meadow, Lynne 85, 101, 106, 156

Meltzer, Milton 16
Merritt, Theresa 152
Micheaux, Oscar 80, 166
Miles, George 51, 54, 56, 58, 64, 85, 108, 169
Miller, Allan 48, 52
Miller, Arthur 22
Miller, Hal 86, 119
Miller, Jonathan 21
Milner, Ron 49, 68, 85
Mimms, Byron 152
Mitchell, Abby 9-10
Monson, Lex 23, 191
Montgomery, Barbara 189
Moody, James 127, 159
Moore, Dudley 22
Moore, Julianne 127
Moore, Melba 156
Moreland, Mantan 171
Morgan, Clark 108
Morgan, Debbi 85
Morgan, JoAnne 15-16
Morgan, Sonny 56, 59, 67
Morris, Garrett 99
Mortimer, Meg 161, 166-168
Moses, Donna 43
Moses, Gilbert 27, 30, 36-37, 41-43, 64, 73-75, 77-79, 86, 99-100
Mtumi, Andre 64, 122, 168
Murdock, George 78
Murray, Albert 55
Myers, Vikki J. 192-193

Nasaba Artists' Management 66, 103
National Black Theatre 50, 61
National Black Theatre Festival 190
Neal, Larry 52, 58, 65
Negro Ensemble Company (NEC) 51, 62, 68, 84, 86, 103, 111-112
Nelson, Jerry 126, 164
Nelson, Novella 151
New Federal Theatre 62, 68, 103, 121
New Heritage Theatre 61, 68
New Jersey Drive 168
New Lafayette Theatre xii, 49-52, 60-62, 66-68, 83
Newman, Paul 17, 79
New York All-City High School Chorus 13
New York Shakespeare Festival 106
Next Stage Theatre Company 14, 20-21, 29
Nicholas, Denise 30, 38, 47-49, 51-52, 74
Nichols, Nichelle 23
Nixon, Agnes 93
Nixon, Pat 127-128, 131
Nixon, Richard 129
Norton, Blake 126

O'Brien, Chester 126
O'Brien, Mortimer 126
O'Casey, Sean 36
Odets, Clifford 118
O'Donnell, Rosie 127
Oliver, Edith 110
Oliver, Thelma 23
Olson, James 21
Olugebefola, Ademola vii, 59
O'Neal, John vii, 27, 29, 34-36, 38, 132
O'Neal, Ron 80
O'Neill, Eugene 21
O'Neill Theatre Conference 103
Orbach, Jerry 149
O'Reilly, Alison Bartlett *see* Bartlett, Alison

Orman, Cheyenne Delores (daughter) vii, 3, 114, 127, 185, 187
Orman, Miles Hunter (son) vii, 113-114, 127, 138, 141, 143-144, 146, 150-151, 185
Orman, Rafaela (grandmother) 172-173
Orman, Rasheda (daughter) vii, 90-91, 104-105, 113-114, 120, 126, 141
Orman, Rochelle "Cookie" (sister) 6-9, 11-12, 113, 182
Orman, Roscoe Irving (father) 4-5, 141-142
Orman, Sharon Delores (wife) vii, 3, 83-84, 86, 88, 103, 105-106, 111, 114, 120, 127, 141-144, 150, 185-186
Orman, Solana Joy (daughter) vii, 6, 105, 111, 113-114, 121, 127, 141, 150, 180, 186
Orwell, George 141
Osbahr, Carmen 126, 130
OyamO 66, 68
Oz, Frank 126

Pace, Jean 27
Paige, Geraldine 17, 21
Papp, Joseph 85, 106-108, 158
Parker, Herbert 192
Parks, Gordon, Jr. 14
Parks, Gordon, Sr. 14, 181
Party on Greenwich Avenue 48
Patinkin, Mandy 127, 191
Patrick, Pat 59, 61, 64
Patterson, Chuck 104, 121, 189-190
Pearl, Ed 75-76
Pelham, Jimmy 64
Perry, Joe 37, 42, 171
Perry, Lincoln 170-173, 175-179

Perryman, Al 104
Pickens, James, Jr. 156
Please Don't Eat the Pictures 105
Plomer, William 42
Poitier, Sidney 16, 29, 75, 80
Pounder, C.C.H. 108
Pottle, Sam 126
Potts, David 102
Powell, Adam Clayton, Jr. 56
Powell, Moses 56
Prado, Francisco 108
Prendergast, Shirley 176
Price, Gordon 126
Primus, Mark 36
Pryor, Richard 143
Psychic Pretenders, The 57, 60, 67
Public School 54 10, 12
Public Theatre 107-108
Puente, Tito 127

Qamar, Nadi 56, 59
Queeley, Edgar "Eddie" (stepfather) 5, 11, 15
Queeley, Edgar, Jr. "Pancho" (brother) 13, 113
Queeley, Leslie (sister) 11, 113, 182
Queeley, Viola "Baby" (mother) vii, 5-6, 8-9, 11, 15

Ra, Karim 192
Ra, Sun 57, 61
Rahman, Abdul 59
Rangel, Charles 178
Raposo, Joe 126
Rasulala, Thalmus 78, 80
Raysor, Roberta 51, 55-56
Reagan, Ronald 106
Reagon, Bernice Johnson 36
Reagon, Cordell 36
Redd, Veronica 85

Redford, Robert 79
Reed, Alaina 91, 96, 164
Reed, Vishnu 61
Reese, Willard "Walik" 64
Reeves, Martha 78
Regan, Gabrielle 146, 150
Reiner, Carl 19
Richards, Lloyd 64, 103, 151-154
Richardson, LaTanya 156
Rifles of Senora Carrar, The 36
Riley, Clayton 58-59
Roach, Max 14, 127
Robeson, Paul xii, 118, 166, 170
Robinson, Bill "Bojangles" 171
Robinson, Edward G. 77
Robinson, Mabel 104
Robinson, Marty 126
Robinson, Matt 4, 86, 119, 169, 171-172, 174-175, 178-179, 185
Robinson, Roger 78
Robinson, Vivian 122
Rockefeller Foundation 49
Rockwell, Norman 13
Rogers, Fred 187
Rogers, Roy 77
Roker, Roxie 23
Rolf, Frederick 18-19
Rolle, Esther 23, 51
Rollins, Howard 102, 107
Roots 42, 70
Rosen, Abigail 17
Rosenblatt, Roger 178
Ross, Diana 127
Ross, Ted 103
Rotante, Rick 14-15
Rudman, Dave 126
Russell, Charlie 52, 174

St. Frances de Chantal School 12

St. Jacque, Raymond 23
Sainte-Marie, Buffy 150
Sallid, Otis 104
Sanchez, Jaime 22, 108
Sanchez, Sonia 65
Sanders, Pharoah 61
Sanford and Son 93, 142
Sands, Diana 75, 78
Sarandon, Susan 127
Satchell, Larry 9
Savalas, Telly 149
Schaeffer, Maryanne 17
Schechner, Richard 41
SCLC (Southern Christian Leadership Conference) 34, 133
Scott, Hal 23, 65, 102, 104
Scott, Oz 65, 103
Scott, Seret 107
Secret Place, The 99
Seneca, Joe 100, 152
Sesame Street xii, 3-4, 15, 86, 91-95, 99, 105-106, 109, 118-119, 125-132, 134-135, 143, 149, 150, 154, 157-158, 163-166, 169, 172, 175, 186-189, 191-192
Shadow of a Gunman 36
Shakespeare, William 106-107, 109-111, 120
Shange, Ntozake 69
Sharpe, Saundra 84
Shay, Michele 103, 108, 111
Shepard, Sam 174
Sills, Paul 14
Simms, Charles 37
Simon, Lisa 126
Singer, Dulcie 87, 119, 128
Singleton, John 79, 143
Sirens, The 85-86, 175
Sixteenth Round, The 111, 118

Smallwood, Tucker 108
Smith, Ed 52
Smith, Jerome 43
Smith, Hank 175
Smith, Nick 52
Smyrl, David Langston 91, 146, 151
SNCC (Student Non-violent Coordinating Committee) 29-30, 34, 36-37
Snipes, Wesley 143
Son Come Home, A 53
Spinney, Caroll 87, 126, 128, 149, 164
Spirit House Movers and Players 68
Squires, Emily 126
St. Anthony of Padua School 12
Stanley, Karma 67
Stanley, Kim 21
Staunton, Kim 191
Steele, Bob 77
Stevenson, Robert Louis 76
Stewart, Ellen 62, 99
Stickney, Phyllis Yvonne 121
Stone, Jon 4, 65, 86, 95, 105, 137, 143
Stovall, Count vii, 108
Strasberg, Lee 17, 21
Strickland, Bill 52
Striking Distance 168
Stuart, Jan 176
Stubbs, Louise 23, 122
Suarez, Matt "Flukie" 43

Tabori, George 47
Talented Tenth, The 103, 155-158, 194
Taylor, Caleb 138
Taylor, Clarice 51, 78
Taylor, Horacena 112
Taylor, Jacob 138

Taylor, Susan B. 156
Teer, Barbara Ann 50, 61, 69
Terkel, Studs 14
Theater-In-The-Streets 48-49
Thigpen, Lynn 152
Thomas brothers (Jim and John) 154
Thomas, Dylan 22
Thomas, Leon 61
Thomas, Marie 156
Three Boards and a Passion 47
Tomlin, Lily 127, 145
Torn, Rip 21
Toure, Askia Muhammad 58, 65
Townsend, Robert 127, 189
Turman, Glynn 50, 75, 189
Twain, Mark 21, 179
Twenty Year Friends 121, 151
Twin Bit Gardens 107
Tyson, Cicely 23

Ullman, Tracy 127

Vance, Courtney B. 152
Van Peebles, Melvin 74, 99
Vogel, Matt 126
Voight, Jon 22

Walcott, Charles 11
Walker, Alice 127
Walker, Joyce 78, 122, 191
Walker, Ron 53
Wallace, Basil 64
Wallace, Royce 78
Ward, Douglas Turner 51-52, 69, 111
Ward, Dick 100-101
Washington, Denzel 108, 127, 138, 143, 158, 174
Washington, Donald 53

Weldon, Charles 84
Wells, Hunter Edmund (grandfather) 5, 8-12, 14, 20, 50, 73, 143
Wells, Viola "Nanny" (grandmother) 5, 8-9, 11-12, 20, 73, 77, 143
We Righteous Bombers 58, 62, 121
Wesley, Richard 65-68, 85, 101, 103, 155-156, 177
Wesley, Valerie Wilson 177
White, Lilias 146, 166
White, Michael vii
White, Slappy 170
Whose Got His Own 49, 52, 57, 194
Wilcox, Preston 52
Williams, Billy Dee 152
Williams, Clifton 192
Williams, Clarence III 22, 48, 108-110
Williams, Dick Anthony 75, 85, 99
Williams, Frances 76
Williams, Joe 20, 127
Williams, John-John 87
Williams, Louie 59
Williams, Samm-Art 68, 111
Williams, Spencer 80
Williams, Tennessee 41
Williams, Vanessa L. 191-192
Williams, Vince 152
Willie Dynamite 74, 78-79, 83, 93, 100, 122, 142-143, 158
Willis, Bruce 168
Wilson, August 68, 151-154, 192
Wilson, Flip 15
Wilson, Trey 149
Winston, Hattie 14, 51
Wonder, Stevie 127, 156
Wood, Collette 76
Wood, Kelly 19
Woodard, Alfre 143
Woods, Allie 51

Woods, Maurice 101, 103, 108, 119, 165
Worlds of Oscar Brown, Jr. 27
Wright, Richard 166
Wright, Sam 51, 56

X, Malcolm 40
X, Marvin 51, 65

Young, Andrew 30, 40
Young, A.Z. 37
Yulin, Harris 47

Zanuck, Richard 75, 79
Zukof, Billy 37

Index of Photographs

Alice, Mary 180

"Baby Alice" 146
"Baby Natasha" 146
Bartlett, Alison 130, 146
Berry, Kelly-Marie 54
"Bert" 146
"Biff" 96
"Big Bird" 96, 130, 138, 146
Bolling, Gary 51
Bosia, Akosua 155
Bove, Linda 96, 130, 146
Brill, Fran 130
Buckley, Lisa 130
Bullins, Ed 51
Bush, Barbara 137
"Buster the Horse" 96
Buzzi, Ruth 130

Calloway, Northern 96
Calud, Annette 130
Charles, Ray 145
Chipkin, Paul 28
Chipkin, Ruth 28
Christian, Robert 108
Clash, Kevin 138
Clinton, Bill 182
Clinton, Hillary Rodham 130, 182
Collins, Beverly 51
"Cookie Monster" 96, 146
Costley, Robert "Big Daddy" 38
"Count von Count" 96, 146

Davis, Ossie 169

Day, Cora Lee 74
Dee, Ruby 169
Delgado, Emilio 96, 130, 146, 159, 164
Dinkins, David 138

Ellis, Helen 51
Eliot, Marge 100
"Elmo" 138, 146, 169
"Ernie" 96, 146
Evans, Estelle 50, 51

Fenner, Janice 50
Fernandez, Peter Jay 108
Ferrer, Jose 180
Freeman, Morgan 108

Gaines, Sonny Jim 51, 70
Gardner, Rob 164
"Gladys the Cow" 146
Glover, Savion 146
"Grover" 96
"Grundgetta the Grouch" 146

Hawkins, Yvette 51
Hervey, Devin 192
Hicks, Tommy 182
Hines, Gregory 160
Howard, Bette 51
Howard, D.J. 193

James, Peter Francis 108
Jemott, Angel 130
Jo-Ann, Ebony 189

Kampouris, Camille 137
Kaufman, Fran 137
Keiser, Kris 51
Keys, Alicia 181
Kilpatrick, Peggy 51
King, B.B. 159
King, Yolanda 180
Knight, Gladys 145

LaBelle, Patti 159
Lathan, Bill 51, 177
Lee, Will 96 108, 164
Linz, Peter 130
Long, Loretta ("Susan") 96, 104, 130, 137-138, 145-146, 150, 159, 164

Macbeth, Bob 51, 60
Manzano, Sonia 96, 104, 130, 137, 146, 159, 164
Marin, Cheech 160
Mayo, Whitman 51
McCutcheon, Bill 146
McGrath, Bob 96, 104, 145-146, 159, 164
McGrath, Cathlin 104
Miles, George 51
Moody, James 159
Moses, Gilbert 36
Muehl, Brian 164
Myers, Vikki J. 193

Nelson, Jerry 164
Nicholas, Denise 38

Orman, Cheyenne Delores 114
Orman, Miles Hunter 113-114, 138, 144, 146, 150
Orman, Rasheda 91, 104, 113-114, 150
Orman, Rochelle ("Cookie") 6, 113, 182
Orman, Roscoe Irving 5
Orman, Sharon Delores 84, 113-114, 150
Orman, Solana Joy 113-114, 150, 180
Osbahr, Carmen 130
"Oscar the Grouch" 96, 146

Parks, Gordon 181
"Prairie Dawn" 96, 146

Queeley, Eddie 5
Queeley, Leslie 113, 182
Queeley, "Pancho" 113
Queeley, Viola "Baby" (mother) 5-6

Raysor, Roberta 51
Reed, Alaina 96, 164
Regan, Gabrielle 146
"Rodeo Rosie" 96
Rosita 130, 146
Rotante, Rick 14
"Roxie Marie" 146
Ruby 96

Smyrl, David Langston 146
Spinney, Caroll 164
Stone, Jon 137
Stovall, Count 108

Taylor, Caleb 138
Taylor, Jacob 138
"Telly Monster" 146, 169
Tomlin, Lily 145
Townsend, Robert 189
Turman, Glynn 189

Washington, Denzel 138

Wells, Hunter 5
Wells, Nanny 5
White, Lilias 146
Williams, Vanessa L. 192
Woods, Maurice 108
Wright, Sam 51

X, Marvin 51